Leading
Leaders
to
Leadership

✯ ✯ ✯

21 Secrets for Leveraging Your
Way to Greater Success

✯ ✯ ✯

John Fuhrman

A Possibility Press Book

Leading Leaders

to

Leadership

John Fuhrman
Copyright © 2004 by John Fuhrman
ISBN 0-938716-30-1

Published by
Possibility Press

Manufactured in the United States of America

Dedication

To those who have failed and have kept going anyway. Your greatness is still ahead of you. Your perseverance will serve as a leadership role model for many who look up to you. I hope many follow in your footsteps as you journey toward your dreams together.

"**F**ollow your decisions with action—whether things are ideal or not—success comes in the doing."

—John Fuhrman

Contents

"Most people have some leadership qualities and the potential to develop even more. They just need to be nurtured by someone who is already where they want to be—to help point the way."

—John Fuhrman

Chapter One

Why Another Book on Leadership?

"For the most part our leaders are merely following out in front;
they do but marshal us the way that we are going."

— Bergen Evans

L eadership training is a hot topic. Business seminars and training sessions on leadership are conducted around the world. Big corporations, home-based businesses, and those in between are always looking for people who are leaders or can be developed into leaders.

The problem is that leadership training and development is typically centered on what people need to do *after* they find themselves in a leadership position or level. They may have gotten there perhaps because of technical expertise or education, but they probably weren't taught the relationship-building skills so essential for effective leadership. Those people most likely didn't grow up in a leading-leaders-to-leadership environment where they were mentored along the way. As a result, they weren't really prepared for the new role. This inadequacy, of course, tends to perpetuate itself within an organization.

Want-to-be leaders need to associate with leaders who are qualified to help them accelerate the climb to the next level of their business or profession. To develop fine new leaders, the focus needs to be on demonstrating, by example and mentoring, the qualities the want-to-be leaders need to have. They also need to be taught to help others grow more proficient in their leadership qualities and abilities. The mentoring process needs to be duplicated, whereby the leader is always training his or her "replacement" and understands that this is the best approach for ultimate success.

For example, imagine you are a home-building contractor. Would you hire a car salesman, no matter how successful, to be a foreman in building your next new home? Of course not! You would first need to teach him about building homes, and lead him in doing it—so he could gain experience and get good at it. (Just because someone is successful in one area doesn't mean he or she knows how to be successful in another.)

Once the new person becomes proficient at building homes, he would then need to be taught and mentored in how to deal effectively with and motivate the other workers before you would consider making him the foreman. He would then be qualified not only on the technical aspects of building a fine home, but he'd also be able to work with others, create a team, and lead each individual in doing a quality job.

Now if you want to expand your home-building business, you would also need to train your foreman to identify and mentor those who want to grow into being foremen themselves. This would then give you the ability to build more than one home at a time, where other homes could be built without your direct involvement. You would then be in more of an overseeing leadership capacity.

If you are already an experienced leader, consider this a refresher course. If not, consider where you are now and decide where you'd like to go. This book will teach you what you need to do to become a leader so you can get there.

You'll discover the major factors holding you back from your true potential. You'll also learn the techniques you can use to break through barriers, and begin the journey toward how you want your life to be. The process is simple but not quick and easy. It's going to take a great deal of effort, as anything worthwhile always does!

Leading Leaders to Leadership shares that most people have some leadership qualities and the potential to develop even more. They just need to be nurtured by someone who is already where they want to be—to help point the way.

If you want to be fit and have a well-toned body, you can't do so just by going to a gym and having a professional trainer explain how to develop and maintain your condition after you've achieved it. First of all, you would need to become flexible—by stretching and loosening up. You would then start working with small weights, gradually increasing to larger ones, while doing the recommended exercises, until your strength and appearance were where you wanted them to be. After that, you would need to devote time and energy to maintaining the look and feel you've developed, and perhaps going beyond.

Edison said, "I've had a great deal of success with failure." For a long time it seemed like I was the only one who lived that. But I now realize that is what successful people go through. They're consistently overcoming failure and rejection. This book is for those who are looking for the knowledge, hope, and encouragement that says, "If others can succeed in spite of all that they went through, so can I."

Throughout my life, I've failed my way to success, with each triumph removing the residual pain of past failings. Never let failure stop you in your quest for a goal. Failures yield valuable information—like road signs along the way. They'll tell you what didn't work or that you need to modify your plans and take a different route. I hope your journey is shorter than mine, but even if it isn't, that's okay. Great possibilities lie ahead for you when you just keep going.

What Is Leadership Anyway?

Some people think leadership is telling others what to do. But that's not true. That may be loosely considered teaching or dictating, but definitely not leading. Leadership is influencing others by example. True leaders don't tell anyone what to do. They would rather invest their time teaching what they know and showing how it is done—so others can get where they want to go. Most of all, being a leader is about putting others first without regard to the payoff.

You'll read some examples of others who went through their own processes to succeed. It doesn't matter what you want to do. It could be anything from building your own business to going to the next level where you work.

Understand the steps to success which are common to all the examples, but it's most important that *you* courageously move forward, step by step. This will enable you to reach goals, achieve new levels of success, dream bigger, and then repeat the process—creating an upward spiral.

We may never meet face to face. Most likely, I will never know who did or didn't follow any of the suggestions in this book. But I'm confident that those who do will make a difference in other people's lives who, in turn, can do the same.

As you read and after you finish the last page, I hope you feel tremendously hopeful. When you say to yourself, "If that guy can do it, I sure know I can," you'll be on your way. Now go out and make a difference in someone else's life, or even in a lot of people's lives—and teach others to do the same.

If we have the opportunity to meet, introduce yourself to me, look me in the eye, and say, "Man, if you can do it, there's no doubt I'm going to succeed!" We'll shake hands and we'll both know that you will do your best to make a difference—whatever your aspirations may be.

"*Leadership is influencing others by example. True leaders don't tell anyone what to do. They would rather invest their time teaching what they know and showing how it is done—so others can get where they want to go. Most of all, being a leader is about putting others first without regard to the payoff.*"

—John Fuhrman

"Caring about others—without trying to figure out how you'll be rewarded—is the fastest way to achieve wealth and happiness."

—John Fuhrman

Chapter Two

A Mentor's "Famous" Rules

"If a man hasn't discovered something he will die for,
he isn't fit to live."
— Martin Luther King, Jr.

I was at that awkward age—somewhere between believing I knew everything, and not questioning anything my most important mentor shared. He did his best to teach me. He had always supported my efforts, was there when things didn't go as planned, and picked me up when I had to look up to see bottom. He is my father. Without realizing it, he, more than any other influencing factor, is why I'm an author and speaker.

No matter how serious the infraction or how bad my grades were, I was never struck by the big man I called Dad. No, there was always a fate worse than the physical pain from a spanking. My father had a gift for crafting a string of words that made any other punishment unnecessary. His short, to-the-point speeches eliminated the possibility of my offering any excuses for my actions. The words he spoke instilled such guilt in me that I honestly believed I would never even think of straying from the straight and narrow again. There was never any doubt about his feelings toward my behavior.

The Rules

It was during one of those memorable sessions that Dad felt it appropriate to teach me the "rules." He told me they were simple, and following them would make my life great. However, if things weren't going as well as they could, it would be because I had broken the rules. Here we go:

> When you are born, from the moment of your first breath, your parents come first—not you.

That didn't seem fair. Yet, I was certain that voicing my opinion would not have been a good idea. So I kept quiet and listened to him say:

> As you get older, God willing, you'll find someone to love. You'll want to spend the rest of your life with her and work hard to make her happy. To do that, she needs to come first, then your parents, and finally, you.

I couldn't hold back any longer, so I asked the question: "When do I come first?"

Dad could have gotten angry. I suppose I could have even been punished for interrupting. Yet, nothing happened. His expression never changed and he proceeded as if the question never came up:

> When two people love each other, one way to complete that love is to get married and have children of their own. If you are fortunate enough to have that happen, things change. You become happier when your children come first, your spouse comes second, and your parents third.

That was it. He asked me if I understood, and I nodded what I felt was the obligatory yes. However, I had no idea what he meant. All I knew was that I was allowed to leave the room. The "talk" was over.

Years later, I finally got it. When my son was born, I looked at my wife and all I could remember was the rules. I realized I would come in first in life as soon as I put other people and their well-being ahead of my own. When you do what is best for others in your charge, it is best for you too—even though you may not feel that way at the time.

Leading and mentoring requires a new focus—the well-being of others, without thinking about what's in it for you. Share your skills and knowledge with someone else. Caring about others—without trying to figure out how you'll be rewarded—is the fastest way to achieve wealth and happiness.

"**T**here are only two possible outcomes to a decision made today regarding your future: It will either bring you closer to your desired destination or push you further away from it."

—John Fuhrman

Chapter Three

Making a Living or Building a Life?

"Are you learning from your past and building on your experiences to create the future you want?"

— John Fuhrman

I met my wife while we were in high school—nearly thirty years ago. We still hold hands. However, there was a time when things weren't this way. While our marriage was never really in any trouble, it wasn't all we thought it could be either.

What happened? I broke the rules. I was so busy focusing on making a name for myself out there in the "real" world that I forgot on whose world I needed to be focused.

If you break the rules, you can get trapped on a treadmill of misunderstanding. You believe that if you just work harder, things will get better. Most of us get married to be together. But we end up spending more time elsewhere, believing that working harder will make things better.

The key words here are "working harder will make things better." Somehow, it's easy to get caught up in the latest trends and fads. You can get bogged down trying to keep up, and frustrated that you never seem to be able to do so.

Generally speaking, the more you try to keep up with things, the further behind you fall. Things change. That means your focus may need to change—perhaps several times—to reach the same goal. For example, if your primary concern is keeping up with fashion, you need to focus on what "everybody's" wearing. But if you do, you'll become fragmented and lose sight of your priorities.

When I realized that my primary focus needed to be on those I care about most—my family—it was easier to do what was best for them. Once that focus became second nature, an amazing thing happened in our lives—we regained control. Having control is one of the most important elements of happiness. We can achieve our desires once we take control and fix our focus appropriately.

The security we searched for suddenly found us. The values we had hoped to teach our children were now present in the examples we set every day. Our concerns about creating a better life for those we cared about were no longer given a second thought. The key ingredients for a better life were already in place.

Do as I Do

As parents, we are always concerned about how our kids will handle new challenges. We often wonder if we're doing the right things or setting the right example. The great news is that by making certain changes now, for the right reasons, your future can be brighter than you may imagine.

A lot of things in life can be done in an easier and often haphazard way. When time seems to be at a premium, it can be tempting to take such shortcuts—hoping everything will work out.

When faced with tough decisions, the paths you choose and the way you navigate them are the ones your children will remember. And children aren't the only ones who will follow your example. You may be surprised by how many others are observing your choices!

Coworkers or people you are responsible for or leading may evaluate what you do one day and copy it the next—especially if they feel you have some influence on their level of achievement. They may also use you as an excuse if any trouble arises, and blame your example as the reason for their actions—or inactions.

Or, they could take full responsibility for their own destinies—emulating the forward-thinking, compassionate leadership you're showing them. When they notice you meet every situation with other people's best interests at heart—with integrity—they'll be more inclined to respond in kind when similar situations arise for them.

What If...?

Your doctor enters the examining room where you're sitting, waiting nervously. In a hushed tone he says, "I wish there were another way to break this to you, but you only have six months to live. Unfortunately, there is nothing I can do for you. I'm so sorry."

Is that scenario stirring some thoughts? What if it were true? Would you spend your remaining time repairing things you've done haphazardly? Would you endeavor to make right the things you've regretted doing or saying? Or would you continue living just the way you have been all along—perhaps ignoring the opportunities that have come your way? Makes you think, doesn't it?

Many of us regret certain things we've done in the past. However, it's often what we've done or haven't done since those events that puts our lives in situations called the present. How is your present? Is it being spent wishing for the good old days? Do you spend a lot of your time hoping for a different future? Or are you learning from your past, as well as every day that goes by? Are you pursuing your objectives, while increasing your knowledge and understanding? Are you building on your experiences to insure the future you want will be there when it becomes the present?

All situations have one thing in common—how you handle them is under your control. You decide, every day, what you're aiming for. Sure, life has unexpected challenges, but you've made all the choices about how to respond to them. This has largely determined where you are right now. Pleasing or not, where you are in life and where you are going is based on the decisions you make every day.

We all need to have a destination in mind when it comes to running our lives. For example, in what business or profession do you want to invest your productive energy? Are you doing that now? Where do you want to be financially when you give yourself the option of not working as much? Are you progressing toward this end? How do you want to spend your retirement years and when do you want them to begin? How would your ideal retirement look? Take a moment now, close your eyes, and imagine your answers.

The decisions you make and the actions you take today will determine your tomorrows. There are only two possible outcomes to a decision made today: It will either bring you closer to your desired destination or push you further away from it. If you don't believe it's that simple, the next time you need to make a decision, ask yourself which of these two outcomes will result, then act accordingly.

For example, suppose retirement timing for you is a money issue. When you save a certain amount, you figure you can quit. Now imagine you are about to purchase something. It's not essential, but you'd like to have it. Would it be best to pay cash, go into debt, or delay buying it?

I'm not suggesting that you always need to do without things that would give you pleasure. If you've been working hard and you've earned above and beyond what you need to live, you may deserve a little reward. But ask yourself some questions anyway. Would charging a one-week vacation on your credit card, that would take you several years to pay off, bring you closer to being able to retire—or will it delay things? What is most consistent with your goals? What would a leader do?

Asking questions like those may cause you to do something you may not have done in a long time. They may spark your creativity and get you thinking about other ways to spend your vacation. If you like the outdoors, maybe you'll do some inexpensive camping. Perhaps you'll visit some people you haven't seen in years, stay with them, and then reciprocate. You'd both save money, and you would have given them a great example to follow.

Perhaps you could use your vacation time to find a way to generate extra income—so you can get out of debt and enjoy future vacations without jeopardizing your savings. Once you get on this track, just keep doing what you did to earn the extra money. Keep it coming in, and you'll shorten the time to retirement!

Various solutions to the challenges facing you will reveal themselves when you take a moment to consider what you're doing and ask yourself some key questions. Get into this habit, and commit to the outcome you desire. It can lead you to attracting others into your life who also want to achieve greater success—and you'll reach your goal even faster. Now wouldn't that be great?

"Once you take action, even if it's only a single, small step, you've set things in motion."

—John Fuhrman

Chapter Four

Pebbles in a Pond

"Definiteness of purpose is the starting point of all achievement."
— Clement Stone

In 1995, I decided it was time for me to write a book. I had been through a lot of ups and downs in my life, overcome a lot of obstacles, and felt compelled to write it all down. I thought others could benefit from what I had learned along the way.

I spent the better part of the next year sending out my proposal, focusing on all I would do when the contract came in. The trouble was I kept sending it out, but all I got back were letters of rejection—many of them form letters! No checks, no contracts. Eventually, because I was constantly focusing on the book instead of my consulting job—that disappeared too!

The concept was simple: Write it, sell it, and get paid for it. It wasn't rocket science. Yet, for the life of me, I couldn't figure out why it wasn't working like I thought it would. Then someone helped me sort things out: I had been confusing simple with easy.

It was a simple concept alright, but the process wasn't easy. The results I desired were certainly possible, as long as I did the required work. But I fooled myself by believing a few measly hours of work would generate a lifetime of income. Unfortunately, I had no real mentors to ask or examples to follow. So, when I didn't get the results I wanted, just like many other folks, I looked elsewhere to cast blame.

I found myself *justifying*—that's when you virtually live life backwards. You look at where you are, say your behavior was okay, and then plan your future. In my case, it went like this: I had written a proposal to sell a book idea. Not one publisher expressed any interest! I justified that all those who had rejected my work obviously didn't appreciate who I was or what I had to offer. I wasn't going to write another word until *they* came to *me*!

That's when I got caught in a downward spiral. To show what I thought was strength, I displayed stubbornness and ego. But I had shut down the very process that would have made all the difference. By refusing to write until they came to me, I only hurt myself. No one knew who I was, and I began thinking no one thought it would be necessary to look for anyone like me. Success was not going to come knocking at my door.

It wasn't until someone asked me what I would do if a publisher said yes. All of a sudden, the light went on in my head. Would I be ready? Did I have something to share? Was I able to effectively communicate through the written word? Sadly, the answers were no. I wasn't ready to be discovered, so I began preparing for that day.

Motion Is More Important than Motivation

I started writing again, not for "them" but for others—sharing from the heart. Interesting things began to happen. Ideas that were previously difficult to come by and put into words now flowed onto the pages.

Suddenly, I received a call. It was a publisher who liked a feature article I had written for a major sales magazine. It was about handling rejection. He actually rejected my original proposal, just as the others had, but—because of the article—he asked if I might be interested in writing about rejection. I had certainly experienced a lot of rejection as a car salesman, which caused me to grow to the point where I became a sales consultant to car dealerships. That's how my first book, *Reject Me—I Love It!,* was born. It's now several books later!

My success had very little to do with how I felt about my ability. It had everything to do with my willingness to do whatever was required to write a manuscript that could fulfill a need to help others. A positive attitude, and a dream or objective, are essential to focusing on a direction. Commitment and appropriate action stir the pot. Consistently doing something in that direction, adjusting as you go, is the only thing that can give you the results you want.

I am usually classified as a motivational speaker, so meeting planners can determine if I'm appropriate for their events. Yet I always tell my audiences that I hope I don't come across as one. I'd rather influence them in a more down-to-earth, funny, empathetic way. I'd rather encourage them to take even the smallest of actions to get rolling, rather than to leave the room uplifted and do nothing. Once they hear my stories, they know that if I can succeed, in spite of all my foibles, they can too.

If you remember nothing else here, remember that, "Motion is more important than motivation." How good you feel, in and of itself, does little to help you accomplish your goals—especially if your feelings come from your response to someone or something external. While a good attitude is essential, it is only one ingredient in the formula for success.

Think of something you'd like to have or accomplish. Now, imagine you're at a convention run by your company or organization. One of the speakers delivers a message that makes you feel tremendous—you're almost walking on air. You go home feeling great, but do nothing different. How much closer are you to your objective?

Imagine that same convention again, but this time you're not particularly struck by any of the presentations. Nonetheless, you take a step toward your goals and dreams as a result of that convention. Regardless of how you're feeling the next day or how negative your coworkers may be on what's a typical day for them, *you* take another step. Even if you're having a challenging day, you still take another step—and another, and another, and so on.

Consider those two examples and what you'll do to motivate yourself long-term. Wouldn't it motivate you to see your goal getting closer? Isn't it possible that if you just keep doing what you're doing, you'll get the result you want? Doesn't it make sense that working on what you are striving for is the best strategy for staying motivated? Focus on the prize, not the price, and it'll keep you going.

The Ripple Effect—*Motion Makes Motivation Materialize*

Have you ever seen a beautifully calm pond? If so, I'll bet you've also tossed a stick or stone into it—just to see the ripples. Have you ever tried to stop them? Of course not. It can't be done.

Once you take action, even if it's only a single small step, you've set things in motion. But you need to take that first step. Go ahead. Risk it. Take a chance at failing. Even if you do, you'll be closer to your goal than ever before—you know what doesn't work!

No matter how much you anticipate seeing ripples, unless you toss something into the pond, there's no chance they'll appear. Conversely, on your worst day, even if you can barely lift your arm, ripples begin when you simply drop a pebble into the water. And they still won't stop until they reach the other side!

Once you see the effect, you know all you need to get started on achieving your goal. Just keep tossing pebbles, that is, taking steps, until you create the effect you desire. As you see the ripples expand, you'll realize that when you throw in a big rock, you can accelerate their growth. The rock is heavier, and your arm will feel the resistance. Yet your commitment to the effect you're after, and the progress you're making, will give you the extra strength to throw as many of them as fast and as high as you can.

You'll also observe that you don't have to toss the rocks as high as you tossed the pebbles to create the same effect. In fact, you can miss your target and still have the new ripples catch up with the old ones. Doing whatever it takes to get things in motion in your business or profession will be more exciting than you may now imagine. Motion makes motivation materialize.

Every step you take toward your objective helps you realize that no matter how small the effort, you're still closer to where you want to be than you were. It helps keep hope alive. It's also easier and more fun to take small steps and continually repeat the process. Planning how to take one giant, seemingly impossible leap, but staying in the wishing-planning-never-acting mode for the rest of your life, is not a good thing. Someday becomes a new word called never.

You'll also be encouraged by the fact that you can repeat this process every day. Even if a middle step is met with failure, you're not sent back to the beginning. Isn't that great? If, because of impatience, all you want to take are giant leaps, you'll actually lengthen the natural learning process that stems from taking smaller steps. A mistake could put you back to square one. You haven't made the incremental progress and experienced the growth that occurs by taking small, in-between steps. The fear of knowing that could keep you from even attempting the goal. So be patient. Take a giant leap by making a series of small steps. Start today.

"While it is always important to be thankful for everything we have, it is devastating to our chances of success to become complacent with where we are.

—John Fuhrman

Chapter Five

The Numbers Don't Lie

"When you're through changing, you're through."
— Bruce Barton

Look back over the last few years and ask yourself if you've missed any opportunities. How did you originally hear about them? Were they explained well? Did you understand what you were being shown?

Now consider this. If you doubled a penny every day for 30 days, you'd end up with about 5.3 million dollars. It's a mathematical fact. No matter how much anyone may argue, the numbers don't lie. It's a simple geometric progression. But what happens when you put people into the equation?

Some People Argue with Logic

Let's say you tell 100 people you will pay them in the above-mentioned way for 30 days. You know it works, because you've already done it. And as a leader, you've shared how it works with them. Here's what would probably happen:

The first day of the program everyone is excited about becoming a millionaire like you. They all start working as hard as they can. However, at the end of the day everyone gets just a penny. There are a few grumbles, but then they remember the millions awaiting them at the end of 30 days.

As they begin the second and third days they find much of the same. All their work is producing minimal results. At the end of the third day each has four cents. Half of them look at the four pennies in their hands, believe what you have is too good to be true, and quit. That leaves you with 50 people to do the work of 100.

The fourth through the seventh days are a bit more difficult because each person left is now doing twice the work. Very little progress has been made and at the end of the first week, each of the remaining 50 has accrued 64 cents. Some won't like it that they are now being paid a single person's share while doing twice the work. Half of them quit. The beginning of the second week finds 25 people left.

As they work through the second week, more progress is made, even though each person is now doing the work of four. They have put out a tremendous amount of effort, and by the fourteenth day they have each accrued a total of $81.92. Some of them will look at all they had to do to earn that small amount, decide that it just isn't worth it, so half of them quit. Rounding things off leaves 13 people.

As they begin the third week, things begin to change. All of a sudden there is obvious progress being made. By the end of the week, each one has accrued a total of $10,485.76. For many of them, that's the most money they had ever seen at one time, and they are grateful. However, there are some with sour attitudes who say it's about time they were really paid for their efforts. They just want to go and enjoy the fruits of their labor, so seven more quit. That leaves six.

As the fourth week begins, those who stuck it out are amazed at what is happening. Everything is starting to come together beautifully, in rapid fashion. In fact, they can actually see the end of their tasks. For those who remained, the total paid to each of them by the 28th day is $1,342,177.20. Put yourself in their shoes for a moment. Have you have ever said, "If I had a million dollars I'd...."? Half of the remaining group did just that, so they quit. Now only 3 people are left to handle the work of the final two days.

If you've followed the math you'll realize that on the last day each of them would have amassed a total of $5,368,708.80. That's an unbelievably large amount, you might say. Yet, when you do the math, you know it is certain to happen. Guaranteed! But if it's such a sure thing, why do you suppose only three people stayed until the end to collect?

It's probably for the same reasons that less than three out of a hundred people ever achieve significant success. Can you spot the reason in the above example? Go back and read it again. Did you notice the one thing all those quitters had in common?

The reason so many gave up is why so few people ever achieve their dreams or objectives. They simply lost focus on their desired destination and followed the crowd. They concentrated on the challenges of the moment and got stuck there. Instead of focusing on the cumulative results they were after—even when those results were guaranteed—97 percent of them quit! Amazing, isn't it?

Being a leader is the way to ultimate success, and almost anyone can become one. But to do so, you need to have the desire to become one. As the saying goes, "You can lead a horse to water, but you can't make him drink."

Emotion Makes Commitments

In the previous example, and in many other examples of success I've witnessed over the years, it is the emotional involvement that keeps people going. This is especially true when things get a bit rough. There are a lot of people with quitter's habits who are all too familiar with giving up—they've done it countless times themselves. They usually quit before they even really get started. So how can those with that kind of track record support others in persisting until they achieve *their* dream or goal? They generally don't and may actually encourage others to give up! Association with such non-leaders makes it more challenging to continue unless the person observing them has a strong emotional focus.

Emotional response is the driving force that dramatically affects our take—our perspective—on any given situation. When we're excited, we want to keep moving to arrive at our destination sooner. If we have a predominating fear of the unknown, we often look for ways to avoid the situation. Regardless, it's our strongest emotion that drives us in the direction we ultimately take.

This is the primary reason that having a strong dream or goal is such an important ingredient to success. Without a dream or goal—a destination you're passionate about—it becomes easy to lose sight of why the tasks leading to its fruition are worth doing. Without something to go for that you really want, what's the point of working harder than you normally would?

Let's bring this a little closer to home. How do you feel about your job? Do you focus on all the things having the job means for you and your family? Do you dwell on the lifestyle it has enabled you to have? Or is your focus on merely arriving at Friday in one piece to collect a paycheck, breathe a sigh of relief, and go home?

The answers will establish your attitude, which determines where you end up. The choice is yours. You can choose your destination and strive for it, step by step, which will improve your attitude and make it much more likely to accomplish. Or, you can let whatever happens happen, and settle for whatever you get.

If you choose the latter, you're not alone. In fact, it's likely that more than 95 percent of the people you know are making that choice as you read this book. Many of them could become leaders, but they have settled in to settling for. It's a dangerous place to be, especially when someone has higher aspirations. While it is always important to be thankful for everything we have, it is devastating to our chances of success to become complacent with where we are.

In business, as in life, there is no status quo. You are either moving ahead by consistently striving to improve your leadership, or you're falling behind, telling the world and yourself you're doing okay or that you just don't care. Either way it's your choice. Lead yourself to where you want to be rather than falling prey to the naysayers because you lack focus on a worthwhile goal or dream. *If you are unwilling to lead yourself to making a change, you've already reached your maximum potential.* And you won't be able to lead anyone else!

If you've worked hard toward a worthwhile objective and achieved it, you deserve to enjoy the rewards of your success. On the other hand, if you plan to continue as you always have, you might as well not complain about how things are or wish how you'd like them to be. When you sincerely want things to be different enough to take a stand, and get either "mad" or excited about them, you'll do different things. When you have a specific goal in mind and are diligently pursuing it, you are creating constant change. Continuously make adjustments and overcome obstacles as you go. That will help you stay on course.

Focus on something you really want. Otherwise, many changes could actually take you further from your desired destination. When aiming for something specific, it's easier to make the right adjustments. This encourages you to follow through with any tough decisions because you know where they will eventually lead to your goal—and it's worth it to you.

"Learning all you can about what you do is important; but caring about people and learning how to serve are the keys to lasting success."

—John Fuhrman

Chapter Six

The Four Cs

"So long as there is breath in me, that long will I persist. For now I know one of the greatest principles of success; if I persist long enough I will win."

— Og Mandino

Dale Carnegie, in *How to Win Friends and Influence People,* tells us to avoid the three Cs: "Don't criticize, condemn, or complain." There are many excellent reasons *not* to do these things but there's a fourth C I feel is also important to share. It simply takes too much time and does absolutely nothing to bring you closer to your goals. In fact, it pushes you further away from them. Before we get to that, though, let's take a look at heroes.

Our view of heroes seems to have changed over the years. When I was a boy, heroes were leaders—people you looked up to and wanted to emulate. You believed they had accomplished admirable things, and you wanted to do likewise. They could have excelled in sports, business, space travel, politics, engineering, science, or anything else you may have aspired to do.

Today, it seems, many want their heroes to be more like they are. Instead of celebrating their accomplishments, some may look for as many faults as possible in order to bring them down to their level. Some may criticize them so they feel better about their own lack of achievement.

I prefer my heroes to be more skillful and accomplished than I am, so I can be inspired to emulate them by doing something on the scale of what they've done. How about you?

Fear of criticism causes many people to pull their heads back into their proverbial turtle shells and shelter themselves in mediocrity. Rather than risk being ridiculed for leading themselves into doing something special, they keep themselves stuck in day-after-day sameness—just surviving.

Then there are those who wholeheartedly invest their time leading and helping others achieve their objectives. They may ask for nothing in return other than asking those they've helped do the same for someone else. They don't seek credit or recognition, and often achieve significant success because of their giving ways. They have found an arena where they can pour their hearts and souls into serving others while enjoying the process. They become servant-leaders—the greatest leaders of all.

When you find someone like this, do your best to become acquainted with him or her. If appropriate, ask for that person's help. But beware of the fourth C. This is a difficult C to avoid because, chances are, it's being done all around you every day. The media does it. Local organizations do it. Perhaps even your coworkers or associates are involved in it. Regardless of how often you may have done it in the past, though, when you are serious about creating a better life, you need to live without it.

So what is the fourth C? *Comparing* yourself to others! Never compare yourself and your own perceived lack of accomplishments with someone who is where you would like to be. One pitfall to comparing is using faulty judgment. Most of us don't have close to all the facts—there is always more than meets the eye. Someone may appear to have done something of distinction with relative ease. Yet, the truth be told, they persisted through tremendous odds to get to the leadership perch where they now sit smiling.

Those striving for the same objective might give up or change directions, thinking it should be easier than what it is. They give success a meager effort but continue shifting directions to what appears to be easier—if it doesn't fall into their laps relatively quickly. It's very difficult, if not impossible, to arrive at a desired destination when people keep shifting the way they're going, in an attempt to avoid the challenges. They'll just keep going off course and never grow into leaders. People only want to follow someone who's going somewhere.

I'll use myself as an example: When someone introduces me before a presentation, my accomplishments are read before the audience. As I come on stage, I'll often ask the audience if anyone would like to do what I do. After all, speaking looks glamorous.

Many people either clap or raise their hands to let me know that, sure, they'd love to be where I am. They've made a comparison and judged that where I am is better than where they are. Some have even decided, without any research, that there is no way they could ever do what I do. So they figure they might as well stay where they are and stick with what they are doing, or maybe think of something else to pursue—something seemingly less daunting.

All those thought processes stem from a single question following a brief introduction. No one bothers to find out if the information presented is even true. Yet they are willing to base serious life decisions simply on what they heard. They may even assume I am smarter than they are, which is hardly the case. What if they knew the rest of the story? Would their answers still be the same?

Would they still want to be in my shoes if they knew that before I sold my first book, I worked on it for over a year—with no income from it? Would they still want to be in my shoes if they realized the challenges my family and I went through while I pursued my dream?

In a large group there are always a few who say yes—they have the conviction to pursue their dreams and goals, whatever it takes. They are open enough and take to heart what I have to share and go for it. I can definitely help them by sharing my story. Then there are the others—not quite sure of what they can or want to do. These people are often new to the idea or haven't accepted the reality that they can do something different—and have a better life.

Follow Your Decisions with Action—*Whether Things Are Ideal or Not*—Success Comes in the Doing

Once you make a decision to separate yourself from the pack, you need to guard against being too careful. Realizing you need to do something different is a giant step toward successful leadership. But it doesn't end there. Here's a little riddle to clarify what I mean:

Q: Three frogs are sitting on a comfortable lily pad, and one of them decides to jump into the not-so-warm water. How many are left on the pad?

A: Three! Deciding to jump into the water and actually jumping are two different things.

Many people have *decided* they want to change their lives, and they may even plan ideal solutions for the remaining time they have on the planet. They want the benefits of change, but they also want to avoid the possibility of discomfort in the process. That's the stumbling block. Change will probably be uncomfortable! Keep in mind the words of Greek biographer and essayist, Phtarch: "Courage consists not in hazarding without fear, but being resolutely minded in a just cause." Leaders take action.

If You're Not Willing to Make Mistakes and Risk Failure, You've Already Reached Your Maximum Potential

So, where are you now? As harsh as it may sound, if you're not willing to risk failure, you've already reached your maximum potential.

Many people interpret that to mean that if they are not willing to risk failure, where they are in life is as good as it's going to get. While that's certainly true, let's look at it from another angle.

Let's use money as an example. Suppose you came to the conclusion that once you've set aside enough money, you'll be able to devote most of your time to your family, traveling, and other pursuits. To accelerate that process, you worked extra hard and took advantage of an opportunity to generate additional income. This could be in working overtime, building a home-based business, or getting a second job. No matter how you look at it, you're risking that what you're doing won't work.

Let's say you've also invested your money in a recommended mutual fund to grow your nest egg faster. It's possible that risk could result in the loss of some or all of your money—the investment could mean failure.

Because you've risked failure on a couple of fronts, and worked harder (and smarter) than others around you, you achieved your goal and reached a point of financial security and maybe even total freedom. Would you still need to keep your money in the same investment? Will you still need to work the extra hours? Probably not.

The money you've earned and invested could well be put into a secure investment that would pay you an ongoing amount sufficient to maintain your lifestyle. Since you've decided to spend more time with the people you love most, would you risk the money you've accumulated? Would you risk an investment failure? No way.

In this case, risking failure would not be the thing to do. Because of earlier risks you took, you've reached your chosen maximum potential and can now enjoy it without worry. Here, it is okay *not* to risk failure. You got to this point only after commitment and dedicated work. If you wish to go to a new level, the risk process would need to begin again. That's okay too. In fact, it's advisable to do so, especially as a leader.

When I was doing car dealership sales training, I used certain phrases over and over again to teach effective selling. After doing hundreds of training sessions and repeating the same ideas thousands of times, I thought I had it right. Unfortunately, that didn't go very far in teaching new people the proper sales techniques. I had only given them examples of what happens when everything goes well.

Many of them went back to their companies and began practicing. They often said that when they got good at those lines, their careers would take off. It wasn't until years later that I realized what a disservice I did them by insisting they get it right the first time. Yes, you can improve your presentation when you practice giving it by yourself. But until you share your presentation with others, you really can't grow. You need to get out into the arena where the people are who need to hear your presentation. They will all respond in different ways to you, making for a learning experience you can't get when you're alone.

Successful leadership comes from the willingness to, at first, do something incorrectly, face the consequences, make adjustments, and do it again—until you get it right. Do your best to learn everything you can about your particular product, service, opportunity, or whatever you are offering. But being able to repeat all the information perfectly is not a prerequisite for getting started. Just because you don't know everything, don't let that stop you. You'll learn as you go.

Memorizing and practicing the "script" by yourself simply creates an emotionless recitation of what you've committed to learn. It never gives you the experience of being sincere and empathetic toward the person or people with whom you are sharing. That relationship can never work—no bond can be developed—when you are simply repeating memorized phrases. This only demonstrates that you are doing nothing more than trying to push what *you* are offering, regardless of what they want or need.

Care About People and Learn How to Serve

When you have learned all you can about what you are presenting, it's easier to have the confidence to listen to people's wants, needs, and concerns. Then you can respond kindly and intelligently, with accurate information that will be of specific use to the person or people to whom you are speaking. But, let's face it, you may need to get back to them later, or correct yourself as you go. It's more important that you care about them and take action to be helpful. As Benjamin Franklin noted, "Well done is better than well said."

When you have a helpful attitude, others are more likely to feel you are looking to solve *their* problems and satisfy *their* wants or needs. Therefore, they are more likely to be forthcoming with all the information you need to serve them properly. Gee, when it comes right down to it, if you can't help them, you may need to refer them elsewhere. That's a kindness that will long be remembered. Maybe they'll look you up later, when the time is right for them.

The only way to make steady progress is to focus and take action toward your destination and, incrementally, each goal you need to accomplish in order to get there. To achieve those goals and have the income you desire, help others reach *their* dreams and goals, by showing them how to overcome their obstacles. It will *never* be just about you! You only get rewarded as a result of successfully helping others.

Learning all you can about what you do is important, but *caring* about people and learning how to serve are the keys to lasting success. Those who have reached the highest levels of leadership realized that early on and, more important, did something about it. They led by setting a good example and helping others win. That's how leaders win.

Since public speaking is listed as the number one fear for many people, I'm frequently asked how I overcame it. I really enjoy what I do, and I desire to make a positive impact on others. But, early on, it was a willingness to fail miserably in front of a group that gave me the courage.

I'm often asked to share how people can overcome their fears of public speaking and turn them into positive power. To do that effectively, I endeavor to set an easy-to-follow example. In the beginning, I decided that, in spite of my nervousness and fear of failing, I was willing to go out and risk falling on my face. I let go of trying to be perfect. People would see I was willing to risk a poor performance rather than cower to the shadow of fear—letting it paralyze me. It takes courage to be a leader, and courage can only be exhibited in the presence of fear.

As I grew, so did my speaking goals. I wanted audiences to realize that if I could achieve success by facing my fears and doing it anyway, so could they. I committed to leading by example and exposing myself to potential failure whenever I did something new.

"Set a good example and help others win. That's how leaders win."

—John Fuhrman

"*Successful leadership comes from the willingness to, at first, do something incorrectly, face the consequences, make adjustments, and do it again—until you get it right.*"

—John Fuhrman

Chapter Seven

What About the B Students?

> *"Sometimes it is not good enough to do your best;*
> *you have to do what's required."*
>
> — Winston Churchill

O nce, while speaking at a student assembly, I wanted to demonstrate the most powerful ingredient for a successful life. If I simply told them to help others and, in the process, they would ultimately be helping themselves, that would not have been convincing. They may have heard that before. I needed to create something the students could relate to and actually see themselves doing.

Unfortunately, I didn't realize this until I was part way through my talk! So, I took a deep breath and this is what I said: "You've all been honest with me so far. I'd like to ask a question, hoping you'll give me an honest answer. How many of you are getting Cs on your report cards?" Many hands went up. I continued...

"Leave your hand up if you would like to turn those Cs into Bs without doing any extra school work." As you can well imagine, most of the hands stayed up. I knew then that they would participate in my plan. So here's what I said ...

"Go find some D students and show them how to get Cs!"

Not surprisingly, *everyone's* grades went up. Please understand, my background is not in education; I simply believe in the laws of human nature. You cannot help others without also helping yourself—it's simply not possible.

Had I told them to study harder or go for extra help, I would have been like every other adult, saying exactly the same thing since *I* went to school. Instead, I shared with them the same principles I tell people who want to go to the next level in their job, business, or anything else they may do.

Have you been focusing on others? Are you giving the best you have, both personally and professionally? As an aspiring or developing leader, change your focus to serving others.

Help enough other people and, in the process, you'll get where you want to go. If you need to modify or completely change what you are doing to reach your objective, will you do so? You may already have the good fortune to have an opportunity to assist others in achieving their potential. If so, keep doing it over and over again and you'll be amazed at the results. Consistently focus on and take action to serve others above and beyond what is expected, and your success will be virtually automatic.

"You cannot help others without also helping yourself—it's simply not possible. As an aspiring leader, change your focus to serving others."

—John Fuhrman

"*If you teach some-one to be average, and that person is an excellent student, the best he or she can be is average. Yet, by setting the bar higher and teaching someone to excel, even the average student is likely to surprise you with how well he or she does.*"

—John Fuhrman

Chapter Eight

Teach Others What You Want Most to Learn

"As iron sharpens iron, so one man sharpens another."
— Proverbs 27:17

A re you training your replacement? As mere mortals, we are on this planet for a relatively short time. However, we can make a difference by sharing our knowledge and experience with others. No matter how permanent we may feel in any aspect of our lives, our place here is only temporary. Our legacy is measured by how much we have cared about others, the difference we have made in their lives, and how well we trained our replacements to carry on after we are gone.

Whether we take an active role and are consciously training our replacement or not—we are, nonetheless, training them. People are, perhaps unconsciously, making mental notes of what they see us do, and often live their lives accordingly. This may surprise you, but it's true. We are all role models—

good, bad, or indifferent—whether or not we realize it or want to be so.

Take, for example, your job. What if, early on, you began training your replacement? Right from the beginning, you start showing him or her everything you do, and how and why you do it. You work diligently to teach that person effective decision-making skills—the keys to supporting and encouraging others, and when delegation is appropriate and when it's not. What do you suppose the results of your efforts could be?

Anyone worried about job security would probably be concerned that the boss might get rid of him or her and have a fully trained lower-paid replacement. Therefore, this is not something in which such a person would be likely to participate. The fear factor would loom too large. Consequently, and sadly, the best he or she can hope for is a continuation of the same old thing.

For the rare few with good attitudes, though, the possibilities are virtually endless. A promotion may be denied because there is no one trained to do the job of the person seeking the promotion. You could eliminate that negative possibility by having your replacement ready when the time comes for you to move on to the next level.

When you train someone to replace you, he or she not only has the chance to learn from you, but perhaps teach you something too. Given that you're working well together, productivity goes up. You both become more valuable employees or associates. That *could* make your situation more secure—although nothing is guaranteed.

If you teach someone to be average, and that person is an excellent student, the best he or she can be is average. Yet, by setting the bar higher and teaching someone how to excel, even the average student is likely to surprise you with how well he or she does.

Class Participation

Sharing your knowledge can also go a long way in reinforcing and increasing it. Like investing your money properly can increase your net worth, helping others with your knowledge can pay long-term dividends.

Encourage your people to think together and share their knowledge. Focus on learning as well as teaching. Invite people to contribute their ideas and solutions and then ask them to improve upon their initial thoughts.

A Pitcher's Dream

My son, John, is a pitcher for his high school baseball team. But to pitch well, even at that level, requires more than just showing up for regular practice sessions. It also demands focusing on the task at hand, coupled with the self-discipline to consistently and independently work on the mechanics of pitching motion. This is done not only to fine tune skills and prevent injuries, but also to increase the ball's speed. It can be a very tedious aspect of the sport since it is usually done in solitude in front of a mirror, but it is essential for all pitchers' success. These efforts can pay off in winning the game.

Have you ever had high-school-aged children? If so, you'll probably agree that they generally had a lot of things going on. They frequently had studies to prepare for getting into college, extra-curricular activities, socializing, practices for more than one sport, and maybe even a part-time job. That scenario made it difficult for them to be consistent at such a seemingly mundane task as watching themselves perform in the mirror.

One day I had the opportunity to watch John as a budding leader, out in the neighborhood with a group of the younger, smaller kids. Because of his size and age, they all flocked to be around him. He was giving them pitching instructions and they seemed to listen better than if their parents had told them the very same thing. Later, I spoke to him about this and asked if he had enjoyed it. When he told me that he thought it was fun, I got an idea to eliminate his boring pitching practice routine.

A good friend of mine was coaching a little league team and was getting ready to begin practice for the kids who were on the team the previous year. I asked him if he could use some help with his pitchers. As anyone knows who coaches kids, all help is welcome! When I told him my son could possibly assist him, he was excited.

The kids were great. As soon as this 6'3" young man walked in with his baseball glove on, they all quieted down. They saw someone who they already looked up to, and he was going to demonstrate how to throw fastballs so they could get more strikes. He was also there to teach them how to think like a pitcher. But first, he had to show the kids the proper arm and body motions so they could throw hard without hurting themselves.

Normally, these drills would be boring. But the kids were excited to have my son take an interest in and help them. John enjoyed having these little kids stare at him, wide-eyed, and listen with amazement as he threw fastballs they could actually hear whiz by.

He worked with every child—making corrections and demonstrating how to do things the right way. They benefited from John sharing valuable knowledge that many would normally not get exposed to until they were much older. At the same time, John was actually working on his own mechanics and became an even better pitcher. He also developed more leadership skills. After all, he was sharing with kids who respected him and wanted to do well, and he wasn't about to lead them astray. Showing others how to do things better always helps the leader.

By the time the season started, John was throwing harder than ever. Even his coach was curious about this vast improvement. Because of helping the kids' team, John had started working out sooner that year. His extra concentration on pitching mechanics, which was intensified by his teaching, had propelled him to a new level of proficiency. He benefited tremendously from helping others become more proficient at a skill *he* wanted to learn. That's how it works— help others and you'll help yourself too!

"*When you study anyone who has achieved extraordinary success in any area, you discover that he or she has failed many times. These were not just random failings of no consequence. They were events that were evaluated to determine what adjustments needed to be made. The world generally sees only the end result.*"

—John Fuhrman

Chapter Nine

Fail Your Way to Success!

"Only those who dare to fail greatly can ever achieve greatly. "
— Robert Kennedy

What would it take to help you feel more successful? More recognition from your peers? A certain amount of money in the bank? More time enjoying your family? Vacationing at nicer places for longer periods of time? How about living the lifestyle about which you've always dreamed? Any of those could be measures of greater achievement. But how can you get to where you want to go in the shortest period of time?

Are you doing new things in your efforts to make faster progress? Or are you pretty much entrenched in your old, established routine, afraid to venture out and possibly fail?

If you're not experiencing lots of failures, you probably aren't doing much! Failing is an integral part of life— especially when you consistently strive to learn, grow, and stretch for new levels of success. Victory comes by making adjustments after each failed attempt, until the desired result is achieved. What keeps most people from accomplishing their objectives is that they don't persist and make enough of the right adjustments along the way. Upon encountering an obstacle, they quit—letting it foil them from their goal rather than using their ingenuity to eliminate it or work around it.

Now, what if people do keep on going, at least to a certain extent, and use reasonably good sense in making appropriate adjustments? What often stymies their completion of the task? The answer is speed—or rather—lack of speed.

One hundred publishers turned me down before I signed my first book contract. The average writer quits after the tenth rejection. If I were to come face to face with those writers and ask if they would ever let ten negative responses control their lives, all of them would probably say no. So then, might their words be different than their actions? Again, the answer relates to speed.

If I would ask them about receiving ten negative replies, they would undoubtedly think in terms of getting them at a pretty rapid clip. They would envision themselves getting through those rejections as quickly as possible, and then getting on with the business at hand. However, when it comes to how they actually operate, that is not what they do to pursue the vision of locating the right publisher. You'd think they had taken slow, painful-process "pills"! They drag it out.

Many writers send out one proposal and wait. And wait. And wait some more. After about two or three months they may get a response. More than likely, especially if they are unknown, it's negative. So they send out another one. A similar period of time goes by and the same results occur. At that rate of response, nearly two-and-one-half years may pass before their point of reference changes.

Instead of looking at being turned down by only ten publishers, they begin to feel sorry for themselves. They think about how hard they've worked over the last two plus years. They incorrectly globalize their results by saying that *no one* is interested in what they have to say. Unfortunately, many of them let go of their dream of being a published author and choose to pursue something they perceive as being easier. But once they encounter bumps on their new path, they quit again. They typically look at the few who persist long enough in their writing or other endeavors to get positive results, calling them lucky.

Looking back, I can now say that I survived and flourished because of speed. At the proposal submission pace of most would-be authors, it would have taken me nearly 25 years to get 100 rejections. I chose a different pace. I sent out two to four proposals every week and had a signed agreement within a year. I wasn't just looking to see how many answers I could get. My focus was, and still is, on finding people who say yes. The number of noes I need to go through to find such people is irrelevant. I just keep on going, no matter what the quest is, and you need to do the same. That's what a leader does.

Failing for the Masses

People sometimes rise to positions of leadership because of a perceived success—not necessarily because they exhibit leadership qualities. Many of them have even failed quite regularly, often resulting in their making adjustments and repeatedly renewed attempts. Admittedly, this is admirable. Sometimes they even come up with better ways of doing things. But that still doesn't mean they are good leaders.

True leaders, from the day they assume the role, perhaps without realizing it, are training their replacements. Those with greater aspirations, who are associated with leaders, watch their every move. What a leader excels at, as well as what he or she does poorly, becomes marvelous training material for leaders in training.

A mistaken belief held by some leaders is the assumption that the best thing they can do is to always get it right in front of their people. Certainly, go ahead and do it correctly when you believe you know the best way to do something. However, when attempting anything new, do not belabor the situation, overanalyzing it as you look for the perfect approach. Instead, go with your instinct as you make the initial effort.

As a leader, the best example you can set for others is to believe in yourself, and do the work necessary to achieve your objective. Realize the possibility of failure, but keep going anyway. Thinking and planning are necessary, but they can't get anything done. It's not even a solid faith in your ability that takes you to your destination. Success comes *only* in the *doing*.

But, even more important than the simple daily doing of whatever it takes, is the humble willingness to fail in front of others. True leaders do that well as they get their egos out of the way. They understand that no person or plan is perfect, and that nobody is a big deal.

Few things of any magnitude go without a hitch—it's just part of the game. It's essential to accept and overcome the hurdles inherent in the process of achieving. Leaders, of course, need to work through people, as well as technical and logistical difficulties. But one of their greatest attributes is a willingness to risk failure. When it happens, they simply get up, dust themselves off, make adjustments, and go for it again.

If you feel the need to find the perfect solution—where you'll have both comfort and accomplishment—you'll just waste your time. And that's not a good thing, since time is running out for us all. Once it's gone, it's gone. There is no way of recovering lost time. However, there is a way to *shorten* the time it takes you to reach your goals—be willing to make mistakes!

Think about it. Venture out while understanding that you'll probably make mistakes along the way. Widen your horizons by learning something new that interests you, even though you'll make some mistakes. Get started and then take action. Boldly go with what you've got and don't let yourself get hung up on the details. You'll learn as you go.

Venturing forward this way certainly increases the odds of making mistakes. But it also accelerates your chances of succeeding. Take advantage of the biggest benefit mistakes can give you—knowledge of what doesn't work.

Let results teach you what you need to correct as you go. Then you can take further action, perhaps altering your course. If things turn out as expected, or maybe even better, your example teaches people the value of trusting their instincts, and increases their confidence in making decisions. If the results are less than anticipated, again, by example, teach them to make the necessary adjustments and move on. The key here is *not* to give up on the initial idea as long as you believe it's a good one.

The value in failing and regrouping, rather than quitting, reveals itself as you get back up and go after your goal again. Failure can be the greatest teacher when you look for the seed of good in it, and apply the sometimes hard-won lessons. By keenly observing what didn't work before and adjusting accordingly before your next attempt, you will shorten the time between the idea and the accomplishment.

Ultimate failure occurs only if you let ego get in the way of humbly going after your objective again, saying things like, "I tried that once, but it didn't work." Just giving up—perhaps fearful of looking foolish—only leads to losing. If you abandon the idea, even though it's still what you really want, and move on to something else you think will be easier, you are creating a failure mentality and habit pattern. You also risk showing others that one attempt is all any goal is worth.

Do you want your people to give up so quickly on their goals? Do you want to reduce the importance of goal setting and make the status quo seem more valuable? Failure is an event to be used as a learning tool, but failure mentality is a sad state of mind.

When you study anyone who has achieved extraordinary success, you will discover that he or she has failed many times. They were not just random failings of no consequence. They were events that were evaluated to determine what adjustments needed to be made. The world generally sees only the ultimate success.

Since you were little, you've probably heard that you need to learn from your mistakes. That great advice often gets buried under our fears and insecurities. We often forget about it and get stuck in the planning stage, so we won't make mistakes in front of others. We become obsessed with striving for perfection and paralyze ourselves with the fear of doing things wrong. This thwarts our ability to move forward with our ideas.

Those who risk failure courageously put their best efforts into the preparation stage and take action as soon as possible. More important, though, they expose themselves to potential success. Such brave individuals often attract key people into their lives who can advise them on how to improve upon and better present their ideas or how to proceed in taking action most effectively. Instead of going through a lot of trial and error, they're able to get to the right ideas or solutions a lot sooner. Those who laboriously analyze the potential of their concepts often stay in the comfort zone of their homes or offices.

This is often called "paralysis of analysis," and it can stifle anyone from reaching his or her potential. People agonize over the variables and torture themselves about the "what ifs." They never realize the tremendous feeling of accomplishment in completing their projects.

"Those who risk failure courageously put their best efforts into the preparation stage and take action as soon as possible."

—John Fuhrman

"**K**eep your energy focused on your goal, investing in yourself and others, until you succeed. Then go for something bigger."

—John Fuhrman

Chapter Ten

The Greatest Investment in the World

"The best investment is in the tools of one's own trade."
— Benjamin Franklin

What makes the stock market go up? What triggers people to buy certain toys for their kids? Economists call it supply and demand, but it's really a form of the law of attraction. People are attracted to whatever they perceive as being beneficial to them. Their perceptions are formed, largely, or in part, by watching what others do.

For example, a new company starts selling a large number of shares *after* one or more major investors have bought lots of shares. The credibility and actions of the initial investors creates a bridge of trust to the new company. This pulls other investors onto the scene. The stock starts going up. If the large investors sell off, generally the rest of the shareholders follow suit. Does this tendency have much, if anything, to do with the company? Sometimes. However, it's often simply a matter of people being attracted to following the actions of the leader investors, with little regard for what the company is really doing.

So what attracts investors to get involved in the beginning? Usually, it's what they perceive as the owner's or company leaders' actions. For example, if they believe top management has shown serious commitment and put everything they have into making the company work, the investors may, at least, take a look at the potential. However, if none of the owners or managers have much at stake, it's difficult, at best, to attract outside investors.

Even if you are employed, you are, in a sense, a corporation. The stock you trade is your ability to reach your potential. When you decide to do whatever it takes to achieve something, and start taking action, you can attract people who can help you reach your objectives. They'll be willing to work with you because you are taking action toward accomplishing a worthy goal.

Such people often had others help them succeed. They, recognize the efforts of someone who is doing things to make a difference. They realize that the improvement of their own lives is a direct result of helping others.

If you decided to build your own business, would these principles apply? Suppose you opened a restaurant and decided to wait for something to happen. You didn't purchase any food, didn't hire any employees, and didn't do any advertising or mention your new business to anyone. You just continued your daily life as if nothing had changed—because nothing did! As a result, your business could be the best-kept secret in the world.

Do you see investors flocking to help you? Of course not. Therefore, it's safe to assume that the business will not survive for very long. It's also likely that when it fails, you would probably blame everyone and everything, except yourself, for its demise. Most people, instead of taking responsibility, do just that.

But, what if you were excited about your new business? You start inviting everyone you come in contact with to visit.

Most people won't show up. Others will come once or twice. Then there are those who make coming to your restaurant a weekly event. Another few come in every day. You incessantly promote your restaurant. Soon, happy customers are also promoting your restaurant and bringing friends and family along.

The difference between the two business owners is obvious. The person who does what it takes to succeed attracted others who can help speed up the process. However, the one who does nothing attracted no one. If you don't invest in your own success, how can you expect others to follow you?

Solid Investments Pay Big Dividends

What if I told you that in order to achieve the success you want, you needed to go to college five times? Would you commit to doing that? Or would you justify where you are in life and keep settling for whatever comes along?

Imagine me telling you that in order to attain your goal or objective you would need to commit to sharing information with 100 people. Would you say you don't know that many people? Would you then retreat to the "security" of the status quo? Would you lose your desire? Would you just be thankful you don't have it as bad as so and so down the street? Would you excuse yourself from the success you want?

What you may be doing is looking at the enormity of achieving an end result and feeling overwhelmed. Significant results represent cumulative efforts and are without time limits. No matter how long it takes, you win whenever you reach your goal. Every step you take toward the goal puts you closer to where you want to be—even if that only means you know what doesn't work.

You need to look at end results as payoffs for long-term investments. Reaching goals requires small and continuous contributions. Understanding this helps you keep going until you reach your goal. As soon as you take the smallest step possible, the process begins, and your possibilities begin to come into sharper focus.

For example, if you read a good personal development book just 15 minutes a day, in the course of your lifetime you could acquire the equivalent of five college degrees. Such books would help you grow as a person, and inspire, educate and motivate you along the lines of the goals you're looking to achieve.

So, let's rephrase the earlier question: How would you feel if I told you that in order to achieve the success you want, all you need to do is invest 15 minutes a day reading the right books? The end result is the same but which one seems more doable?

Investing time in helping others achieve their wants and needs is the way to realize our own. This can mean doing almost anything—depending on what method you've chosen to achieve your goal. If you are an author and speaker, it would entail providing the best books and programs you possibly can, to assist the readers and audiences in getting what they want. It is only in serving others that we can increase our prosperity.

Here's how it works. Let's start small. You invest in others. You find a person or company you can help to achieve a goal. It could be as simple as fulfilling a product or service need. Or it could be as grandiose as helping someone achieve something major like building a dream house or setting themselves up financially. You begin changing your focus from just your own goals to making certain this individual or that organization achieves its desire. You commit to helping them, whatever it takes.

When you repeat the process, there will then be two people or organizations you've helped. The third time you go through this process, you'll be gaining momentum and building a successful track record and good reputation. Yet, all you've seemingly done is help one more person or organization. As you go along, you look for others you can help, while also requesting referrals. Word of mouth is spreading that you come through for others. You get a raise, a promotion, or reach a new level in your business. Your sphere of influence is growing. You're beginning to experience how helping others can work for you. You're becoming a leader.

The most important thing about this process wasn't mentioned. I deliberately left it out—*time*. I never showed you how long accomplishing your end result could take. Why? It doesn't really matter. As long as you accomplish it, you win. If the result you achieve is major enough, you may even be living a life that is better than anything you may have ever expected.

It's a lot like selling books. To become a bestselling author, you first need to sell the most important book of your life—the first one. Nothing can happen until the person who has the desire gets the process started. Take that first step. You'll not only be closer to your goal; but, no matter what happens, you'll never be further away from your end result than you are at that very moment. Keep your energy focused on your goal, investing in yourself and others until you succeed. Then go for something bigger! It's all part of becoming a leader.

"Ultimately, it's the dream that drives us to take one more step toward the objective or life we desire. It is the one step that makes those who take it so much more excited and full of anticipation than the average person who has simply surrendered to the daily grind."

—John Fuhrman

Chapter Eleven

Where the Dreams Are

> *"All people of action are dreamers."*
> — James G. Huneker

My garage is usually a mess. But I don't think much about it until I need to find a certain tool. Then I lament over its sorry condition and often begin to believe that the all-important tool is missing or stolen. Sound familiar? Do you ever find yourself putting off a project because the job cannot be completed without that tool?

Is it possible you may even begin to justify, that is, make excuses about why that particular project is not as important as you once thought? Might you even then see what tools you can find and create a project that you *can* do with what you have available? As you begin doing the project you settled for, and begrudgingly feel as if this is your lot in life, imagine stumbling across that special tool. Then what?

Do you start getting excited? As you look at this seemingly invaluable tool, you feel a growing desire to do the original project, don't you? You develop outright enthusiasm for tackling the job. You drop the project you settled for and begin your originally desired task with great pleasure. You may even feel a sense of renewed comfort, knowing that something you thought was missing or stolen was there all along.

Dreams are a lot like that. We often let the ones that once excited us slip away or get buried under life's pile of everyday activities. Sometimes when we lose them it's easier to move on to doing something less desirable rather than finding the misplaced dream. As events and challenges fill our lives, it's even possible to forget we ever had the dream in the first place.

People who let go of their dreams are often easy to identify—just listen to their excuses. They may tell you they stay at jobs they hate because of the benefits. They complain about things at work but wouldn't dream of making a change. They go to great lengths justifying why it's worth being dissatisfied with their lots in life. Have you ever done that? Have you ever held yourself hostage to the status quo? That's not leadership.

Can You Get the Dream Back?

What does a dream have to do with leadership? Dreams are the cornerstones to building solid leaders. Without a dream to drive us, it becomes very easy to walk away from a task or life mission. Without something to get fired up enough about to hurdle the obstacles, people can more easily abandon the quest if the going gets tougher than they expected. But they rarely get the joy of overcoming and completing.

Inevitably, challenges come our way that can make it easy to give up. But, a big enough dream or objective can cause a leader to inspire his or her team to plow ahead through tough times. Focusing firmly on the desired outcome, and helping the team accomplish it, stirs leaders to look for solutions to the challenges met along the way. He or she shares the dream, inspires the team to look beyond their noses, and sets an example of purposeful determination. They are beacons to others who want to grow to leadership as well.

Do the following the next time you find yourself in a situation where you don't have enough money to do something: Instead of giving up and saying, "I can't afford it," use the leadership skill of creativity and say, "How can I afford it?" Just those few words can change your mindset and get you thinking about ways to achieve something, rather than giving up before you start.

Ask yourself how you can do something, and put yourself in an open-minded, resourceful state. Your mind assumes it can be done even though you haven't yet figured out how. Instead of looking for an excuse not to achieve something, you begin looking for ways to make it happen. Exercising your mind that way will strengthen its ability to find solutions rather than excuses. Ideas will often come to you that will produce results better than you ever anticipated.

Beyond Your Wildest Dreams

Have you ever been asked if you'd like to succeed beyond your wildest dreams? How would you answer that? Can you even consider what would be beyond your wildest dreams? To make something like that happen, one key factor needs to be in place—you have to have wild dreams!

That concept is so simple that most people overlook it. You cannot accomplish anything without first thinking about it. Consequently, to ever achieve anything extraordinary, you at least need a wild dream as a reference point. Otherwise, how would you know what to stretch toward?

The reason many people don't achieve anything significant is because they were taught only to go after something realistic, reachable, and attainable. Sure, you want your intermediate steps to your final goal to meet those criteria. But for your ultimate goal, that is sheer nonsense. Just getting to the end of each day, collecting a paycheck, paying your bills—all with little excitement or anticipation—what kind of life is that? Those are all "realistic" alright. Surviving another month on the job, or losing a few pounds is certainly reachable and attainable. But, you may be asking, "Is that all there is?" No, no, a thousand times no!

On July 21, 1969, history was made. Man landed on the moon. For those of you old enough to remember, you can probably picture exactly where you were. What a great moment in our lives. But for me, the understanding of setting outrageous goals—shooting for the moon, so to speak—occurred eight years earlier.

The fuel wasn't developed. No rocket was powerful enough to do the job. There weren't even people appropriately trained to pilot the mission. Yet, U.S. President John F. Kennedy stood before the world and stated that, by the end of the decade, America would put a man on the moon. Which part of that was realistic?

Realistic is whatever you believe! Wasn't it JFK's ability and courage to share and pursue his dreams that made his country look to him as a leader? Wasn't it his ability to set goals and stand by them with conviction that kept the citizens' confidence high when obstacles came along?

Dream big and encourage others to do the same. Listen to what is on their hearts and minds. Help them discover their dreams. Do whatever you can to support and guide them in achieving their goals. In doing so, you will find leadership becoming a more natural, pervasive part of your life, and you'll be more likely to accomplish those wild dreams.

What if You or Those You Work With Haven't Yet Found a Dream?

You may be someone who has been burying your dreams so long that you've given up the quest. Or you may know someone in that situation. One thing that may help you find your dream is to nurture the dream in someone else. Observe and feel the excitement and passion as he or she describes a treasured dream. It may help you move some of the "baggage" you have been using to unknowingly bury your dream over the years. It might reveal something special inside you that you haven't seen in a while.

Who would you look for to find a dream? Would you take a chance that they may not be able to find theirs either? If I were you, I'd find myself a sure thing. I'd look for someone I know who has a dream. Do you know who the best dreamers in the world are? Children. The younger they are the bigger they dream.

The best view can be attained by getting to eye level with your dreamer. That could mean kneeling down and looking right into their eyes. Ask what his or her dreams are and wait for the answer. This will stir you to start remembering your goals and dreams and the hopeful feelings that go along with them. As you continue to look at and emotionally connect with the child, imagine how the little boy or girl would feel if you said to stop dreaming because he or she can never have what they want. Most of us couldn't do that!

Now picture the dreams you had as a child. Focus on how wondrous and hopeful you felt when you thought about being a great athlete, a top actor, an astronaut, or a firefighter. Did you feel yourself burdened with the day-to-day details of going to school, doing chores, or the other mundane tasks of your youth? Probably not. In fact, you may have used your dreams to help you through those daily tasks. They helped you have a happier attitude about the chores you were assigned.

Let yourself have those enlivening feelings again. Look beyond the grind you may be in and let your heart soar. You may need to start fresh to develop new dreams and ambitions. That's great. As you think about and plan how you will achieve them, the everyday-average world around you seems brighter. You are looking forward to something. Routine tasks seem to take less time. Your attitude toward others automatically improves. Those who work around you may even want to learn what you're doing to make it through each day so cheerfully. They may comment, "What's up? You seem different lately."

That's where the dream and leadership come together. You can help those who are around you become better workers and people. Share some dreams with them and ask about their goals and desires. Help them discover what it is to dream again and you may set off a chain reaction. You could end up doing something great together—a project or business association that sweeps everyone to a higher level.

You may suddenly find your leaders looking at you in a whole new light. It could even lead to an unexpected promotion or a raise in pay. How would you feel about that? If nothing else, the power of having dreams and doing what it takes to achieve them helps you do your work, without resenting it or trying to cut corners just to say you've finished. Your disposition is brighter.

You may even realize a new self-confidence. You're encouraged enough to give the required effort to your career, or business, or the new project you've wanted to start. Instead of wondering what might have been, you dedicate time and energy to it with a new determination to succeed. You begin attracting people into your life with whom you can happily work, as you march toward your dreams and goals.

Having and pursuing dreams is what separates the winners in life from those who just get by. It only takes a dream and the hope of achieving it to bring about a more positive outlook on life and your future. Use this as an incentive to do what it takes to find your dream and commit to it. Ultimately, it's the dream that drives us to take one more step toward an objective or the life we desire. It is the one step that makes those who take it more excited than those who have surrendered to the daily grind.

Are You Doing "Okay"?

If you're still not convinced of the importance of dreams and their relationship to leadership, consider the alternative. See yourself as someone who has no dream—someone who sees where he or she is as where the situation will stand for a long time. Can you feel the weight of it all bearing down on you? It doesn't feel very good, does it?

Often, in an effort to "take the weight off," you begin to justify the situation. Instead of looking to make things better, you begin telling yourself how this isn't so bad or that you don't have a choice. After all, many others have it worse. The trouble is, that kind of thinking will actually make the weight seem even heavier. To relieve yourself of this new pressure, you may even begin convincing yourself that you're actually satisfied with the way things are.

Do you find yourself telling others that you're doing okay? If someone has achieved some success, do you label them as "lucky"? Do you look at others who are achieving their dreams as materialistic or greedy? These may be signs that you're trying to protect yourself from seeing that you have no dream to pursue. Perhaps you'll recognize these as warning signs. If you've experienced them, you may need to look really hard for new dreams.

I spend a lot of time discussing the importance of having a dream with virtually every one of my audiences. I've lived on both sides of the fence. I spent many years doing "okay," wondering why I was miserable. Then I risked the unknown and started pursuing my dream. The life I have now came after tremendous risk and sacrifice, and I love it.

Two of the greatest benefits of going through obstacles to get to where you can live your dream are the knowledge you'll gain and the personal growth you'll experience. When faced with a challenge, you know there is always a benefit on the other side. Setbacks are seldom permanent. Your potential to succeed only increases the odds in your favor, as long as you persist. Embrace obstacles when they come, and break on through to the other side. Doing so will put you one step closer to your dream.

"Inordinate efforts in attempting to ensure smooth sailing result in a lot of planning and procrastination, but very little progress. Go with what you've got when you've got it. Know that bumps along the way aren't going to stop you."

—John Fuhrman

Chapter Twelve

If Not You, Then Who?

> *"He is strong who conquers others; he who conquers himself is mighty."*
>
> — Lao-Tzu

Some people spend a great deal of time pointing at others, blaming them for where they are in life. Seems less painful to them to be in a situation they don't like when they make it someone else's fault. However, that blame can often be the very thing that keeps them there longer than they need to be. When they finally take responsibility, the pain they feel due to the situation may cause them to take the steps necessary to change it.

I often speak at writer's conferences. I tell authors and would-be authors that during the first two years of the release of my first book, I was on the radio hundreds of times, wrote countless magazine articles, and was speaking to audiences all across the country.

Without exception, every time I tell my story someone says they don't have to do that since they signed with a big publisher. That always amazes me. How could anyone who took a portion of his or her life to write something worthwhile turn his fate over to someone who has hundreds of other books to worry about?

I tell such people that the average book sells around a thousand copies and is then dropped to a backlist. I then suggest that since they've already invested a good deal of their past writing the book, they now need to invest some of their present time and effort in making sure the book has a future. In the final analysis, every author is responsible for the success of his or her book. The author is the magic.

The behavior patterns of many authors are just like those of the thousands of other people I've met while speaking at business conventions. They keep putting their futures in the hands of others. Instead of taking control of their lives, they let the economy, government, employers, and even the media dictate how they will live. Many people want someone else to do the work, while they sit around to collect the benefits. They somehow believe it's owed to them.

Risking Responsibility

Leaders take full responsibility for creating their successes—as well as their failures. Their hands are so busy working at achieving goals that there isn't time to place blame. Blaming is only for the weak.

Many people are so concerned about being criticized for what they do that they are unwilling to risk failure. They spend so much time making "safe" decisions, based on what they believe will please others, that they never take the action necessary to accomplish worthwhile goals. They often imagine negative results, perhaps being rejected or ridiculed. The risk of failure looms so large in their imaginations that they won't even take the chance to succeed.

It is a leader's responsibility to take risks and therefore, at times, fail. Failing in front of their people—whether it's family members, coworkers, business associates, or others—teaches them far more than giving the perception of never making a mistake. Getting something done is far more important than constantly planning to get it right and rarely doing anything. Growth and profit are seldom made from great planning alone—they come in the doing. Real wealth comes from executing a plan, while making adjustments, until we achieve the desired results.

A true leader will never say anything like, "We tried that once and gave up when it didn't work." He or she may make an attempt and not get the desired results, but that person makes some changes, fine tunes the idea, and goes for it again. This teaches everyone who is in his or her sphere of influence that it doesn't matter how many attempts you make at a goal or dream. What matters most is that you keep going until the objective is reached. As Thomas Edison said, "Three great essentials to achieve anything worthwhile are, first, hard work; second, stick-to-itiveness; and third, common sense." Don't ever quit.

Don't Change Your Objective—*Just Your Approach*

How many kids want to go to a Disney® Theme Park? Ask a group of kids from the neighborhood and see how many volunteer for the trip. Now imagine telling them that some of them will be flying, others will go by train, and still others will go by bus. Do you think any of them will decide not to go because of the mode of transportation? Of course not.

It's the same in achieving anything worthwhile. The accomplishment does not depend on the method of arrival. There is seldom only one way to reach an objective. As long as it's legal, moral, and ethical, no matter how you get there, your accomplishment will be the same. It won't be diminished if you use several different ways to arrive. The real importance is found in how you grew along the way.

Achieving a goal is almost always based on how well you adjust to challenges along the way, rather than trying to plan a path that is obstacle free. Inordinate efforts in attempting to ensure smooth sailing result in a lot of planning and procrastination but very little progress. Go with what you've got when you've got it. Know that bumps along the way aren't going to stop you.

The only way anyone can hope to achieve something is to first *begin*. Yes, a certain amount of planning always needs to be a part of the overall process. Focus on the dream, and you'll figure out the actions necessary to get from point A to point B. By persistently doing proactive things, while making adjustments as you go, you improve your chances of arriving, more so than if you spent a lot of time analyzing everything. Go with what you have—right where you are.

The dream creates action, leads to more enthusiastic emotional involvement, strengthens commitment, and pumps up the momentum. It also keeps us on track so we can blast through the obstacles. Passion for the objective helps overcome any challenges.

Do You Deserve to Be a Leader?

When you can lead yourself to the completion of a goal, you can also lead others as well. That's what contributes to your creating a truly successful life. Commit to helping others get what they want, and you'll succeed beyond what you might now imagine. Sincerely accept and embrace the possibilities for you to make your dreams a reality.

Many people, sometimes in an effort to stay humble, feel undeserving of achievement. That is especially true if you focus only on yourself and what the achievement brings to you personally. It is easier to feel deserving of the reward or the position of leadership when you realize you benefited others along the way.

When you think of helping others succeed, but feel undeserving of reward, ask yourself who else might be able to help them. The answer is often that you're the right person, in the right place, at the right time. You're qualified and deserving enough to lead them to where they want to go. If you have any doubts, just ask for assistance from those who are leading you.

*"**I**f you want to know the results that continuing to work in your current occupation will produce, look at those similar to you who've been doing it five, ten, or fifteen years longer. If their situations leave something to be desired, you need to make a change."*

—John Fuhrman

Chapter Thirteen

It's Not the Time, But the Steps You Take That Count the Most

"The man who rolls up his shirt sleeves is rarely in danger of losing his shirt."
— Anonymous

O ne of the many benefits of speaking to large organizations is that I get to meet some very successful people—multimillionaires, in fact. They often mingle with the audience and encourage people to ask questions about their journeys.

People ask, "What kept you going through all the hardships and obstacles?" or, "When did you first realize success was possible for you?" and perhaps, "Did you ever think you'd be this successful?"

These questions are answered with patience, care, and understanding so that those asking can see the possibilities for themselves. Successful leaders are caring people who take the task of helping others succeed quite seriously. They keep answering questions long after others might have become annoyed, setting a good example for leaders-to-be to emulate.

But, through all the years and meetings I've attended or spoken at, there is one question nobody asks: "How long did it take you to make it?"

Most successful people realize that time is usually irrelevant. But, when might time be relevant? Is it ever?

Are You Part of a Sad Reality?

Earlier I mentioned that I've often asked people in the audience if they'd like to live as I do and got the anticipated reactions. Then when I tell them what I had to go through to get there, far fewer of them were willing to participate.

Imagine, even when they know the outcome could be tremendous, and exactly what they say they want in whatever the arena is, many still aren't willing to weather the challenges. So how can anyone be expected to go for something when he or she doesn't have a clue as to what the outcome could be? It takes faith. Unfortunately, many people don't attempt much of anything simply because they aren't sure what the outcome will be.

But even when there is proof right in front of you of what you can accomplish, it's still possible to focus on the task and challenges and forget about the reward. That's what makes dreams and goals so important. When you have a change in focus from what you need to do to what you can have after doing it, the challenges seem smaller.

Leaders accelerate their success by helping others find and then focus on their dreams or objectives. When you do this, it's often easier to get those you're leading to take the next step. Show them that what they are pursuing is worthwhile and that relentlessly working for it is the only way to achieve what they want.

Anything worthwhile in life requires effort. Unfortunately, most people aren't willing to make the effort. This may include building fine careers or businesses, being happily married, raising loving children, excelling in sports, and being exceptional leaders. Look at all these things as investments with a huge potential payoff. You'll see that consistent effort over a long period of time is the key to doing your best—to make certain you'll arrive at the destination you've chosen. Who knows? The outcome could be much better and more important than you may think!

Settling In to Settling For

When people find something worth pursuing, they respond in different ways. Regrettably, the most common response is that if it happens, that would be nice. Statements like that are weak and noncommittal. At the first difficult challenge or obstacle, such people justify where they are in life and settle for the status quo.

I call that settling in to settling for. It means getting used to whatever happens *to* you instead of working to make things happen *for* you. It's a trap so seductive that many people fall prey to it. Those trapped into that way of unexciting living will make it sound attractive in order to draw you in too. If they believe you're thinking of doing something special, they try to dampen your spirits by telling you it won't work.

Leaders can't be seduced by the easy-appearing life of complacency that settling in to settling for offers. They believe there is something better out there for them when they work hard enough for it. They realize that the only things instant in life are credit card purchases, coffee, oatmeal, and pudding. But none of them have anything to do with success.

Success begins when you commit to doing more than others and start taking action. As soon as you do, you can tell yourself you're becoming a success. Your commitment and initial effort already separate you from those who are convinced that: "You can't fight city hall," "Life is the same old stuff," or "It wasn't meant to be," or some other losing attitude adopted if something doesn't work out.

While gratitude is an important element of leadership and leading a good life, there is a big difference between gratefulness and complacency. Be thankful for what you have, but move on knowing that you have it within yourself to do better. Don't settle for anything less. If you stop growing, you start dying.

You are in total control of the choices you make. You are not falling into the trap of just living with whatever comes along. You don't rely on good luck to just happen—you create it. While your success may make you appear lucky in the eyes of those who are complacent, you know the effort it took to get there.

You'll Never Be Closer to Success than When You Take Your Next Step

When you take your next risk or accept and begin to overcome your next challenge, you move a little closer to your objective. No matter how small the step, you can see a little bit more of your destination. No matter how difficult the last step was, you've never been closer to success.

Understanding that it takes many steps to complete a journey is only part of what you need to think about. You also prove to yourself and those you are leading that reaching a dream or objective is not only possible but almost certain, as long as you keep taking another step toward it.

Life, in general, is a series of steps. A better life is achieved by committing to and always taking just one more step toward each of your goals and following through. That approach makes even the most seemingly impossible task appear doable. If, after every obstacle or challenge, you focus on the next step rather than the whole rest of the journey, it is much easier to keep going. As long as you consistently keep going, anything is possible.

Understanding that you will achieve your objective by taking the necessary steps is easier than mentally beating yourself up if you need more time than you estimated. Sure, you need to have a game plan and strive for a time of completion; this gives you a track to run on. If you need more time, simply re-set the goal.

Every time you take another step toward your objective, you separate yourself from those who let life's circumstances control them and their choices. You become stronger as you exercise your mental muscles and develop a consistently better attitude. Others will see your example and may ask for your help. Giving it to them will strengthen your leadership abilities and bolster your confidence to realize your objective.

"**C**onsistently recognize and thank those who have helped you, and generously share what you've learned with others."

—John Fuhrman

Chapter Fourteen

My Greatest Ideas Came From Others

*"People are all alike in their promises. It is only in
their deeds that they differ."*

— Moliere

For a while, I've been part of a mastermind group of professional speakers. We are five speakers committed to our success in the speaking business. None of us speak to the same audiences so we don't compete. However, we all have similar challenges with marketing, planning, and the like.

Each month we get together to review recent accomplishments, set new goals, and ask for help as needed. When one of us asks a question or shares a difficulty, we all contribute ideas until we arrive at a solution. This is where the benefits of having a mastermind group are most obvious.

While we all may start out with our own ideas for a possible solution, by the time we finish it's as if there was another person with us. That "other person" is the most viable combination of our ideas. This often results in a new, unique solution that no one would have thought of on his or her own. More often than not, that idea is the best one of them all.

Sometimes when we solve a problem for one of our members, the others in the group experience an additional benefit. That solution, perhaps with some minor adaptations, can be applied to our businesses as well.

Look for Others You Can Help, and You'll Be Helped Too

Just having knowledge is not the key to being a leader. In fact, it is often one of the factors that separate leaders from followers. A follower often thinks he or she has the knowledge needed to be successful. But, a true leader is always learning and humble. He or she isn't afraid to admit not knowing something and then asking for help. A leader knows where to get the knowledge—who or what can be relied upon to provide it.

Leaders who ask for help do more than just get answers to resolve an immediate situation. They set an example for others to emulate. Teaching others that there is no need, nor is it possible, to know all the answers is a valuable lesson to share. Otherwise, people can spend all their time trying to gather an inordinate amount of information rather than moving on with the dream or objective at hand. It can actually be a way to delay the work of taking action. Have you ever caught yourself doing that?

Something else that happens when you ask for help is the sharing of what knowledge you do have with the person you asked. Many people have no idea what value they can bring to others as they generously offer their knowledge and experience to support them. Besides, it's a joy to give. Everyone benefits.

A great example of this occurred at a convention where I was speaking. Another speaker asked if I could give him some marketing ideas. We began to chat about different approaches and what his objectives were. As the conversation went along, he realized the path we were taking wouldn't work for him. As we discussed it further, from a variety of angles, I agreed.

The great result of our conversation was that I got an idea that led to a new market and some new products that had never occurred to me before. I was so amazed at the result that I now look even more for others who might need my help!

Observe the Leaders in Action

While there are many different options to learn various skills, few are as impactful as observing leaders in that arena. As a member of the National Speakers Association, I have the privilege of associating with the greatest speakers in the world.

Some of my associates may criticize these leaders or compare them to others, but my approach is different. I make an effort to appreciate their uniqueness, while endeavoring to learn what makes audiences react as they do at certain points during their presentations. This active observing allows me to better evaluate what I need to do to better satisfy my clients and help them take action.

This technique applies to virtually anything at which you want to excel. When you observe leaders doing what you aspire to do, you can learn volumes. You can then sort out what works for you and what doesn't, as you develop your own unique style.

As simple as it is, many people ignore opportunities for learning by observation. They just barrel ahead egotistically, neither watching the great people in their fields, nor asking for their help. They may think that, just because they've been successful in one area, they can succeed in the new role. This is sad. My experience has been that, when asked to help or teach, truly successful people are willing to share their knowledge and experience. Sometimes they may even assume the role of an ongoing mentor. They find that it not only satisfies their desire to give back, but that it can also improve their skills as they focus on the teaching. The best way to learn is to teach!

Discover this for yourself. Find something you're pretty good at but would like to improve. Help someone who is not as skilled or knowledgeable as you are to develop in this area.

You'll be amazed at how good you feel afterward and the improvement you'll experience in your own level of competency.

The other benefit to sharing your knowledge and experience is that it demonstrates to those around you how long-term success is achieved. As discussed before, consistently helping others reach their goals while creating win-win scenarios can make a leader's success virtually automatic. This is an important aspect of leadership. In essence, by helping others, who in turn help others, you are training leaders. All this contributes to helping you be a more effective leader. It's an ongoing, enriching, learning, and growing experience.

Credit Where Credit Is Due

As you teach what you know, listen to others for their input. You'll gain valuable insights—even from the novices, as they often have fresh new perspectives that could accelerate your success. To encourage this free flow of information from others, you need to be comfortable to be around. One great way to create a comfort level is through expressing gratitude for the contributions that person makes, and giving him or her appropriate credit. Some leaders make a big mistake by not appreciating and acknowledging what their associates have brought to the table. They take all the glory themselves—a definite no-no!

As you practice sharing ideas back and forth with others, you'll come across the missing piece you need to propel yourself to the next level. The source of that information may be a total stranger or someone you've associated with for a long time. However, once you've received the benefits of the idea or suggestion, you need to give credit to the source or catalyst for your recent success. A simple thank you, privately or, even better, in front of that person's leader and peers, will work wonders for both your morale and that of the information giver. You may want to write a note of appreciation or do something else to express your gratitude. Always be generous with your thanks. People need to know they made a difference. By letting others know you appreciate their input, they're more likely to keep you in mind when they have other suggestions or opportunities to share.

Many of you have heard the expression, "What goes around, comes around." It's often spoken in a moment of anger, after someone does something negative to you or someone you know. But it also happens when you contribute to the betterment of someone. The key to it occurring more regularly is to constantly be giving, but never looking for appreciation.

When you expect thanks or repayment for a service you have voluntarily given, you'll probably be disappointed. Most people aren't generous with their gratitude. It's like showing up at someone's house with a gift in hand for the sole purpose of getting something back. If you give something freely and expect nothing in return, you'll never be disappointed. Part of being a superlative, well-respected leader is to be a role model in this area.

It's a great pleasure doing things for others and fun, too, because you'll be looked upon as a leader for taking the initiative. Those you've helped will seek your opinion and often follow your guidance. Surprise repayments, perhaps from another source, will come—and it's fun to never know when or how they're going to happen.

Suppose you gave someone a dollar every day. You probably wouldn't notice any financial impact on your life. Let's say that on the very last day of the year, he or she paid you back. You'd have $365! That may mean a special weekend away for you and your family as a result of doing the little things for others on a daily basis.

Consistently recognize and thank those who have helped you, and generously share what you've learned. You'll notice that after doing this one thing, even for a short period of time, your life will become much better. Gratitude and generosity are keys to a happier, more satisfying life in all areas.

"In striving for your objective, you'll discover hidden strengths and talents you didn't know you had. All you needed to do was look for them. They've been there all along."

—John Fuhrman

Chapter Fifteen

Don't Follow the Followers

> *"Any officer who is afraid of failure will never win!*
> *Anyone who is afraid to die will never live."*
> — General George Patton

Many people who consider making changes in their lives feel overwhelmed at the possibility. Somehow they have come to believe that, in order to improve, massive change is necessary. They think of total change as the only way to succeed, rather than sorting out the positives and negatives of their current situations to determine exactly where change is needed. The natural response is to rationalize (tell yourself rational-sounding lies!) that the status quo isn't so bad.

These people look at their lives historically and come to the conclusion that if they haven't been able to make a significant change up until this point, it just isn't possible. Therefore, the seemingly logical conclusion is to condition themselves to make the best of their situations and be satisfied with their lots in life. After all, it seems to work for others they know. Of course, they've never asked these people if they are truly happy or just grinding it out. People often look good on the outside, but are hurting inside. Things are not always as they appear to be, and many relationships are not deep enough to reveal the truth.

Observing and learning from others has brought me to conclude that the idea of massive change is, in fact, overwhelming. In many cases it seems impossible to achieve—a monumental task. I can understand thoughts about making do with what we have, and appreciate why some people would feel change is a hopeless situation. But remember, nobody's perfect in his or her vision of what can be.

Leadership isn't about perfection. It's about day-by-day working toward success. It's about leading yourself first and then others in the quest. Success is founded on a compilation of events that either you create or participate in creating. It's the victorious adjustment to those events that enables you to arrive at your desired destination.

No successful person I know of has put a size requirement on the changes necessary to make a positive move forward. But some change is always essential. Otherwise, you get the "same old-same old" (so-so) boring experiences. You'll be amazed at how much of a difference even a small change can make. British novelist Arthur Ransome shared: "Grab a chance and you won't be sorry for a might-have-been." Benjamin Franklin observed: "God helps those who help themselves."

An Above-Average Decision

Suppose you wanted to save a million dollars. There are two approaches to this goal. Many people believe the time to begin saving is as soon as they have enough money. Consequently, 95 percent of them retire with little visible means of support. But what if, next week, you have an extra $10 after all your bills are paid?

If you took that $10 and put it into the bank you'd be closer to saving a million dollars than those who are spending their extra $10. You'd then be financially above average. Just imagine. Putting aside just $10 on a regular basis puts you in a small percentage of the population that reaches retirement with more money than most.

The real success comes when you learn how powerful it is to put that $10 aside. It has little to do with the amount, but a lot to do with achieving what you want in life. Once you make a decision (saving a million dollars), and commit to doing whatever it takes to make it happen (consistently setting aside a certain sum of money, as well as, perhaps, doing more to increase your income), simply repeat the process—until you arrive at where you want to be.

Adding on Is the Answer

As I mentioned earlier, people are sometimes under the impression that to change their lives they must tear down everything they've established and start over. This is faulty thinking, and it can discourage them from ever attempting anything new. Fortunately, there is no need to start from scratch every time you want to make a change.

Think of it this way: Suppose you've just completed a new addition to your home. You converted your garage to a great room for entertaining and expanded the old garage area forward, doubling its size. Now everyone in the family could enjoy a relaxing evening, listening to music or watching a movie in a larger, more comfortable room.

But what if you tore down the entire house and started over—just to make the addition? Forgetting the expense for the moment, would all that extra work be worth it? Since the rest of the house is solid and comfortable enough, would tearing it down and rebuilding it make it a better place to live? Obviously not.

Apply that same thought process to changes you want to make in your life. Begin with the existing foundation and "add on" to either strengthen or improve it, or both. Build upon what you already have. As you consistently add small changes to your strengths and skills, you'll grow and reach your objective. Now that's more doable, isn't it?

Even when you were adding on to your house, some things may have hindered making the improvements and would have needed to be torn down. That same rule applies to you personally. Do you need to tear down some walls of resistance to build on your foundation of success? Tearing down those walls to build the "addition" will give you more room to grow comfortably and expand your horizons.

The point is, any improvement, no matter how small, enhances your life. Any change you make to better your life increases your level of satisfaction, and the confidence to tackle something new. Small changes result in small increases in value. Major changes can result in dramatic increases in satisfaction and confidence.

When is enough, enough? How do you know when you've made the changes necessary to achieve the success you desire? You'll know. You may suddenly realize that you've arrived. More than likely, it will happen when you notice that you're no longer complaining about where you are.

One of life's greatest tragedies is when someone has worked diligently, achieves success, and never stops long enough to realize it. That person's life is so out of balance and in habitual oblivion that he or she keeps right on working—never enjoying the rewards of his or her labor. Some people feel that it's wrong to sit back and relax for a little while, after they've reached a certain point. Since you choose where that point is, you have every right to enjoy the rewards it provides. You may chose to aspire to a new dream or goal, as you delight in what you've already achieved.

What Does It Take to Be Above Average?

Everything in our lives seems to be statistically measured. There are studies tracking virtually everything from milk consumption to market penetration. Many of the numbers are compiled so we can be told what to buy, where to live, and how we rank compared with everyone else. I like to think of it as "danger with numbers."

We discussed earlier that comparing where you are with where others are is not a good idea. Nonetheless, many people base a large part of their lives on where they fit within the statistics. This often leads to what I call *cashing in their future* before they have the cash.

Do you know what I mean? If the statistics show that successful people drive a particular type of vehicle, they tend to buy it. Rather than working to achieve success first, which would make owning the vehicle easy, they borrow money against future earnings to have it now. Unfortunately, that lowers their financial position. They'll be driving a success vehicle that's actually eroding rather than representing their true monetary picture.

Today, approximately 85 percent of all new vehicles are financed. But wealthy people aren't likely to do so. One way to be above average is to do what wealthy people do, so you can reach wealth sooner. That might mean repairing your old car. Or it could be buying a used one with cash. You'd then be able to put away money that would otherwise have gone toward making payments on something that is certain to lose value.

When faced with a decision that could affect your future, always ask yourself, "Do I really need it?" or "Would I do it this way if I were wealthy?" For example, if you're considering a major purchase and have to finance it ask, "Do I really need this?" or "Would I pay for it this way if I were wealthy?" If the answer to either question is no, then that could be why you haven't achieved the level of financial security you would like to have. Perhaps you've been buying things you don't need with money you don't have. That's a no-no!

Asking those two simple questions puts you above average. Doing something the majority of people aren't willing to do (for example, repair what you've got, save enough to pay cash, take a challenging job, build a business, or plan for the future) makes you an above-average person. You're closer to the successful life you want and more likely to be on track to get there.

Have you ever spent more time planning for a vacation than planning the rest of your life? Take some time and plan for a brighter future. Draw a map to your destination, and secure your position as an above-average person. Leaders are above average. Otherwise, why would anyone bother emulating them?

In striving for your objective, you'll discover hidden strengths and desires you didn't know you had. They've been there all along but weren't obvious because you didn't need them. Average people never find them. They simply don't need them to continue along the path of sameness.

Now go lead others by teaching them these lessons, and show them how it's done.

"*Leadership isn't about perfection. It's about day-to-day working toward success.*"

—John Fuhrman

"*Once you make a decision, and commit to doing whatever it takes to make it happen, simply repeat the process— until you arrive at where you want to be.*"

—John Fuhrman

Chapter Sixteen

The 95 Percent Factor

*"If anyone seeks for greatness, let him forget greatness
and ask for truth, and he [or she] will find both."*
— Horace Mann

Political polls, surveys, studies—the list goes on and on.
People are fascinated to know what the rest of the
world is up to. Supposedly, the purpose of gathering
such information is to use it toward a positive end. Or, at the
very least, it's to use it to prevent things from getting worse.
Somehow, it doesn't always seem to work out that way.

As mentioned earlier, 95 percent of us who reach age 65
are either dead broke or dead. While that may seem disturbing, it probably won't change much in the future.
Unfortunately, it seems as though most people often ignore information like this, and the same patterns of behavior that
created this sad reality keep occurring generation after generation. What's even more disturbing is that the possibility for
breaking that cycle is almost too obvious.

Simply put, to achieve results that are different from what
95 percent of the population is achieving, we need to do what

the top 5 percent are doing—and encourage those we're leading to do the same.

Dare to Be Different

If you continue to do what you've always done, you'll continue to have what you've always had. Perhaps you've heard that phrase so often that it's become a cliché. If that's the case, you may need to look at it again from a different angle—the perspective of accomplishment.

Suppose you've accomplished what you've set out to achieve. You have your finances in order, plenty of time to spend with those you care about, and the satisfaction that you earned every bit of what you have. Why would you want to change now? You probably wouldn't. Once you discover what works for you in terms of achieving your goals, you simply repeat the process or take the next step, until you arrive at your *next* destination.

However, if your life to this point has been based on years of repetition followed by moanings of dissatisfaction, you may want to consider doing something else. That may preclude what you're doing now, or it may be something you can do in addition to your current occupation.

That's often easier said than done. You've grown accustomed to your routine and there is a certain amount of security in knowing what is going to happen every day, even if it's not to your liking. In addition, many of your peers will try to "protect" you from possible failure and dismay by attempting to discourage you from bettering your situation. In reality, what they're doing is trying to keep a member of their ranks from escaping.

Sadly, many people don't like it when one of their own succeeds. Some say it's jealousy and envy. More often than not, though, it's a case of them finally seeing their own potential and where they'll stay if they do nothing about it. They may be so insecure that they believe the world won't be looking at the one person who succeeds, but rather at those who did nothing and went nowhere.

Your success, in effect, calls attention to their complacency. They would sooner exist in secret boredom and sameness than have one person in their circle succeed and show the others what can be done.

Shed the Dead Weight—*Make Some Changes and Move Ahead*

Have you ever noticed how much faster you can travel when you're carrying a lighter load? Imagine going through life with the added burden of all the negative thoughts that 95 percent of the people on the planet have. According to many surveys, most people hate their jobs and are deeply in debt. In spite of all that, they probably won't do anything to significantly change their lots in life.

On the other hand, judiciously following the practices of the remaining 5 percent can change your life remarkably. As soon as you see your true potential and realize you can reach it, you start losing negative baggage. The pace to achieving change quickens, which, in turn, helps you maintain a positive attitude.

You may be saying to yourself that it couldn't be that easy. However, it's not as difficult as you may think. The main thing is to get started by opening up your thinking to the possibility of change.

Remember this? "If Tommy jumped off a building, would you follow him?"

How many times did your mother or father ask you that kind of question? Why wouldn't you just follow Tommy off the roof? You knew the outcome and decided that wasn't what you wanted. What if 95 percent of the population jumped off a building somewhere? Would you follow them, or go your own way?

Look around. The results of not taking the initiative to lead, while continuing to do the same old things, are everywhere. The clues to the results of your life habits are staring you in the face. Learn from them and decide what direction you'd like to take from here on out.

For example, if you want to know the results that continuing to work your current occupation will bring, look at those similar to you who've been doing it five, ten, or fifteen years longer. If you like the way their lives have turned out, keep going. But, if their situations leave something to be desired, you need to make a change.

That doesn't necessarily mean you can simply walk away. You undoubtedly have responsibilities and obligations. But, if you want more out of life, you can always do something in addition to what you're doing. Or you can take courses to learn something new or make yourself more valuable, which could lead to accelerated earnings.

Take the lead in your own life by doing something different. It's the only way you can possibly produce results that are different and better than what 95 percent of the population does.

"*To achieve results that are different from what 95 percent of the popula-tion is achieving, we need to do what the top 5 percent are doing—and encourage those we're leading to do the same.*"

—John Fuhrman

"Reward the action—not just the result."

—John Fuhrman

Chapter Seventeen

The Difference Between Show and Tell

"More and more people today have the means to live but no meaning to live for."
— Viktor Frankl

G iving is temporary—showing is permanent. Let's say you're on the job and are given an assignment for you and your people. As a leader, you divide the work so that each person has a stake in the completion of the task. You give everyone a deadline and a different time to keep you apprised of his or her progress.

As the accomplishment of the mission moves along, you are faced with two people who are falling further behind with each passing day. Being the leader, it is ultimately your responsibility to see the assignment to completion. Your superiors aren't interested in who did what or who didn't do his or her part. They're only concerned with one thing—the completion of the task within the deadline.

The first person you visit readily admits he doesn't know how to accomplish his particular task. He mentions that if you show him how to do it, he believes he can learn enough to complete the assignment. You consider if there is enough time to teach him what to do while still meeting the deadline. Realizing that this won't be the only task you will ever be assigned, you decide it would be a good investment to teach your co-worker certain skills.

The second worker you stop by to see admits defeat. She is adamant about the fact that she simply, flat out, can't do the task. You could try to teach her right away, but you realize that she will only learn once you convince her that she has the ability to complete the task. But since that would involve a lot more time than you can afford, you simply complete the task yourself.

Your boss commends you for completing your assignment within the prescribed period of time. In fact, you are immediately given another task and promised certain rewards upon its completion. Given the fact that you have the same people to work with, what do you suppose will happen with your two workers?

You invested time teaching one worker how to accomplish his task. It's a good bet that he will do a great job for you the second time and get his part of the assignment done. But what about the other worker? What did you teach her?

Just as the first worker learned to repeat the process he was taught, the second worker will do the same. You've taught her that even if she fails to do something, you'll be right there to do it for her—in order to make the deadline. Not only will it be more difficult to teach her as time goes on, but you'll also find that if she is allowed to continue in this fashion, she'll actually want to accomplish less!

Big People, Little People

Remember when you were a kid? If you got away with something once, you knew you could get away with it again. When an adult finally got fed up and stopped or corrected you, weren't you confused? Of course you were. You started wondering why, all of a sudden, something you thought was okay to do, apparently wasn't.

If that continues to happen, some young people will hesitate doing much of anything new until they are certain it will meet with approval. This conditioning can cause tentativeness and limit growth and maturity. It can stifle creative thinking as well as discourage these kids from taking risks.

That type of conditioning has very little to do with age. Most adults also want to receive approval for what they do. It's human nature. That approval may come in the form of compliments or a paycheck, but it's essential for most of us to continue. Without it, we often retreat into a mode of doing "just enough to get by." If that happens, productivity, morale, and creativity diminish.

Be Complimentary and Supportive

Leaders need to recognize and acknowledge the accomplishments of those they are leading. They also need to see when someone is giving 100 percent effort but is off-track in some way and, therefore, not getting the desired results. Here, a leader can excel first by simply providing enough encouragement and guidance to get the job done. Then the leader needs to give all the credit to the person who accepted the help, modified his or her approach, and went on to create the desired outcome.

Another key trait of a leader is not only the willingness to fail, as previously discussed, but also giving others room to fail. Failure is a great teacher. Unconditionally supporting someone who fails demonstrates the leader's compassion toward that person as a growing human being. Doing this will better ensure that he or she will feel safe enough to be open to listening, and making the necessary adjustments to successfully complete the given task. The knowledge the individual gains during this nurturing process gets deeply embedded, and encourages them to stretch and risk failing again. It makes that possibility seem more like a natural part of the learning process, rather than something to be avoided at all costs.

Standing behind and supporting people as valuable individuals—instead of just as means to an end—reflects one of the major differences between a leader and a manager. Letting people know they are worthy of your support as fellow human beings, and not just based on what they've done for you lately, is a great way to instill the desire to take on more difficult tasks.

What if You Help Others Succeed?

Suppose you had the ability to make the greatest widget on the face of the earth. How successful would you be? Well, if the world wanted widgets and knew you had them, you could be successful. However, your success would depend largely on how many you could produce. If you produced enough, you would attain a certain level of success. But would you have the time to enjoy it?

Now, what if you started a widget company and taught your people how to build widgets as well as you did? Assuming the same demand and production, you'd have success and the time to enjoy it. The quality of your product would make it highly desirable and, since you had others producing at the same level as you, your output would multiply.

What if you made a shift and went one step further? Suppose you took your best producers, taught them to teach others, and set them up in their own facilities as independent contractors? Now, as a reward for your efforts, you would receive a part of their profits which would grow as they grew. Your focus would then shift from producing high-quality widgets to doing whatever you could to help the others be as successful as possible in producing them.

The old adage of "clawing your way to the top" is still an option. However, in many situations, this involves doing things you may not feel comfortable doing or, worse yet, compromising your integrity. As a result, many people choose to stay right where they are. This is why people often fight success. But what they really need to do is maintain their integrity, and either change the situation or remove themselves from it. Some people may also believe that in order for them to enjoy success, someone else has to lose. They might have observed this type of scenario one too many times and believe that's how it's done.

Fortunately, no one else has to lose in order for you to win, and no one needs to compromise his or her integrity. When you sincerely help others achieve their own levels of success, as covered before, the attainment of your goals is virtually assured. Examples of what can result from helping others reach their goals or improve their situations are too numerous to count. You can probably think of some yourself that apply to you and what you are doing or want to do.

Stay true to upstanding values and you'll be more likely to attract others to work or associate with you who do the same. Never compromise your integrity to get ahead. If you do, no one will believe in or trust you, and you'll never be able to lead.

Reward the Action—*Not Just the Result*

Individuals and organizations tend to focus entirely too much on results. While getting to where you need to be is important, you need to consider that there are many ways to get there, and to work intelligently. When the end result is the only focus, pressure may be exerted to avoid the risk of considering what could be wise alternatives, in an attempt to not upset certain individuals or entities.

By taking a different, perhaps unconventional or adventurous approach, you open yourself to more risk. You risk making mistakes and causing delays in reaching your destination. However, you also risk developing new ways to achieve your dreams or objectives, and potentially exceeding your expectations. Here's a classic example of risking failure in order to succeed:

Some years ago a large automotive dealer group hired me to help them increase sales. When I interviewed the salespeople, I noticed that they all carried little binders listing the names of the people they talked to. The prospective buyers had yet to tell the salespeople whether or not they were going to buy any of the cars. More correctly, the salespeople had never asked any of these prospects to buy a car. Their associations with what could be potential customers had merely been friendly chat sessions.

I soon learned that the sales staff was under intense pressure to perform. So much so that if they felt a customer might say no to them they would let him or her leave the dealership and simply file their contact information away. They called it the pending file. I called it the *fear file.*

After spending time with the dealer, he asked if I could help and, if so, how long it would take. He also wanted to know about how much it would cost. I told him $5,000 plus $50 cash and it would take two days. Keep in mind, this was many years ago.

Needless to say, he was taken aback and reluctant to invest that kind of money for the proposed effort. But he was also curious as to what the $50 in cash covered. I explained that he would invest the $5,000 in my services and the $50 would be spent on his people to solve the problem.

He was about to say thanks but no thanks when I made him another offer. If he wanted to see the results first he would need to pay more later. I then offered to take the $50 cash up-front and if I didn't achieve the results he wanted, I would walk away empty-handed. But, if I exceeded his expectations, he would pay me on the spot and add an extra $1,000 to my fee.

He agreed to my second offer. Up to that point, this dealer averaged about 11 car sales a day, or about 300 a month. He wanted to boost that by 100 more sales a month. This man was putting a lot of pressure on his managers to make that happen as well as offering thousands of dollars in bonuses for their achievement of the new numbers.

When a bonus is offered that is a lot higher than the others that preceded it, the psychological impact is that virtually everyone believes the task is unattainable. That certainly seemed to be the case at this dealership. I was confident the $50 cash deal would help them change their way of thinking.

The next morning I met with the entire sales staff of over 50 people. Many of them were concerned by my presence. Every time someone like me had shown up before, that meant massive changes were in the works. The resistance to change was incredibly strong. However, I assured them I wasn't there to change anything. In fact, I wanted them to continue doing exactly what they had always done. I just wanted to add some fun to the day.

That got their attention.

I held up the five ten-dollar bills and asked for a raise of hands if anyone wanted them. After the "volunteers" surfaced, I told them the plan. From that point on, until the end of the day, they were to count all the people who told them no. The person with the most noes would win the $50. All they needed to do was call everyone in their "pending file" and get them to say no!

There was a lot of nervous laughter with many of them wondering if I was serious. I assured them that I was very serious, and tacked the money to the bulletin board for everyone to see. I looked at them and said I would be there until the close of business, to hand the money to the winner. I then let them go.

Without going into the details of the day, the phones were in constant use because the belief that if all that was offered was $50, this had to be an easy task. It was. Each time someone got a no, that salesperson would remove the file from his or her binder.

By the end of the day, about 80 percent of the files were eliminated from all the binders. In addition, the competitive attitude throughout the dealership kept all the salespeople on their toes. I handed out the $50 to the winner and collected my fee, including the bonus.

The dealership owner learned that he would continue to have success as long as he didn't pressure people not to fail and, instead, actually encourage them to do so. By the way, that day the sales staff sold 37 cars—more than triple the norm!

"When you practice the life of a servant-leader, every day can be like a birthday or other gift-giving occasion. When you focus on what you can give and how you can help others, amazing things happen."

—John Fuhrman

Chapter Eighteen

If You Keep Score, the Game Is Over

"Do all the good you can, by all the means you can, in all the ways you can, in all the places you can, at all the times you can, to all the people you can, as long as you ever can."
— Anonymous

I sold my first car way back in 1979, after I had been working at a dealership for about two weeks. It was a 1976 Toyota Celica liftback, and I can even tell you the customer's last name. This was very exciting for me because I thought it would help me make a good impression. I also wanted to make a good living, since I had just gotten married.

During the next nine months, I was salesman of the month four times. Three times I came in second. I went from a low-paying hourly job to earning enough in one week to pay for our first two-week vacation to the Caribbean—with cash. I was earning more each week than many of my friends were earning in a month. Pretty good memories, huh?

One memory I don't have is a single name or recollection of any potential customer who told me no. I can't remember any sales technique that didn't work. And I can't describe a bad day at work.

Don't misunderstand. Lots of people turned me down. At first, many of the approaches I took didn't work. I'm also certain that I had more than my share of bad days. I just never focused on them. My only concern was doing whatever it took to sell enough cars each week to reach my income goal.

If we were given a new technique or sales process, it didn't matter whether or not it worked the first time. If you wanted to keep your job, you continued using it until you made it work. The end result was the only thing that mattered, not how you got there.

One of the things that helped all of us succeed was also my first lesson in leadership. All of the salespeople were in their early 20s (I was 22). Since we came from various backgrounds, we became good at different aspects of any new approach at different times. We supported and used each other's talents until we all mastered whatever we were supposed to learn.

We would take a customer as far as our own abilities would allow. We would then use each other's strengths to help complete the sale, helping each other succeed. The side benefit was that the customers really enjoyed all the attention. Consequently, we all sold a lot of cars.

Everything Can Be a Gift

When was the last time you lent something to someone? Did that individual return it in a timely fashion? Did they *ever* get it back to you? If not, how did you feel? Your feelings may have run the gamut from disappointed to angry, and you may have decided to never lend anything to anyone ever again. But this could be a big mistake if you are looking to become a stronger leader and have a better life.

Who is really affected by the way you feel?

What if that person simply forgot that he or she ever borrowed the item from you? Feeling disappointed or angry isn't likely to make the item magically reappear in your possession. In fact, if you express your feelings in an unkind manner to this person, he or she may withdraw from you and your friendship. Is any possession worth that?

What if that person didn't return it to you on purpose? How would your feelings change things? You may have a very negative effect on the wrong people. If an individual is deliberate in taking an action, expressing how you feel won't necessarily encourage a change of heart. Maybe he or she doesn't care how you feel. So, the perpetrator of the deed would be insulated from being affected by your attitude. The only ones suffering from it would be you and any innocent people with whom you come in contact.

Keeping the two negative outcomes just mentioned in mind, think again of the question I asked earlier. Is there anything in your possession worth either outcome? Probably not. So, how can you avoid these situations? Simple. When you give something away, do so without expecting anything in return. Doing so prevents anything from ever being taken from you. You will enjoy the good feeling of giving without setting yourself up for the potential tension and disappointment if the items are not returned. While many of the things you give out may be returned, the ones that aren't can never be sources of stress.

One of the key traits of leaders is their generosity in offering their time, talent, ideas, or, in some cases, possessions to help others. The simple, thoughtful act of giving sets a tremendous example, one difficult to ignore. By participating in the betterment of others lives, you will be a role model to emulate. Best of all, helping others will help you improve as a person. Everyone wins.

Do You Want to Be "Right" or Save the Relationship?

If you have kids, the following has undoubtedly happened to you. One of your children has had a disagreement with a friend. By the time it comes to your attention, two things have probably happened. First, the original cause has become a forgotten issue. Second, while both kids no longer remember what happened to cause the angry confrontation, neither side is willing to be the first to offer a gesture of forgiveness. Why not? Their egos are keeping score.

Perhaps the conversation with your child went something like this: You say, "Why don't you go tell Jeff you're sorry, and that you want to be his friend?" Your child replies, "He was the one who said the last bad thing about me. He should go first."

I could go on, but doesn't this sound familiar? Kids do it all the time. Unfortunately, I've also seen it happen with married couples, coworkers, longtime friends, and family members. We all remember who got the last word out and that, somehow, is supposed to determine who apologizes first.

As soon as one or both parties decide that the other needs to go first, the game is over. Everyone loses. We all know of someone who hasn't spoken to someone else in years—over a situation just like this. Perhaps you've even commented as to how silly it was. But, before you point a finger, think. Have you ever been in a similar situation?

A leader takes the lead and humbly apologizes, even if he or she believes it's the other person's fault! There is always something to apologize for, even if it's simply, "I'm sorry I offended you when we last talked. I know I got a little loud when you pointed out my mistake." This helps to break down the wall of stubbornness between the two of you, and moves you toward, once again, being able to work together or associate in a peaceable way.

Leaders let go of ego and are willing to be "wrong" — they don't let disagreements ruin their relationships. Putting others first and laying aside our pride shows we care about people. It leads to winning for all and, of course, is a good example for others to emulate in developing their leadership skills.

Every Day Is a Day for Giving

When you practice the life of a servant-leader, every day can be like a birthday or other gift-giving occasion. Focus on what you can give and how you can help others reach their goals, and amazing things will happen. First, you can become incredibly good at what you do. Second, you can also begin attracting others who can really use your help. You'll then accomplish more and start realizing a life of greater significance.

Many people say they fear death. But I think the real fear comes when they believe they may die without having accomplished very much. No one wants to die for nothing, yet so many spend their lives looking for something with which they can make a difference. It's unfortunate that it's often right in front of them, but they just don't see it.

Earlier, I mentioned about a man who thanked me for writing *Reject Me—I Love It!* as though I had written it just for *him*. When he gets to the point where he can help others through their rejection challenges, his life will have reached a new level of contribution.

Everyone who is impacted by something positive you say or do gives your life more meaning and significance. In response, some people may give you a hug, a phone call, a letter of appreciation, a thank-you card, an email of gratitude, an invitation, or even gifts on occasion. But don't expect it. Most people generally don't take the time to do it, even though they would like to. They need to grow more before they understand the importance of showing appreciation.

Tenfold Surprises

It's been said that what you give will come back tenfold. Sadly, many don't believe that. They may go out to give, but base their giving on what they anticipate receiving in return. I've even seen some people actually calculate exactly what they expect to receive based on their "gift." The trouble with this attitude is that the "gift" is really an investment, not a true gift.

True givers seek no return. They give unconditionally, without expecting anything back. They even give anonymously, or through third parties, so their donations cannot be traced. As a result, their prosperity grows. That's just how it works.

Because I delight in simple examples and solutions, I began offering what I could, without calling attention to myself. I just followed the examples of the great leaders and success stories that came before me. The results have been nothing short of extraordinary. I am now able to choose where I feel I can have the most impact, without anyone knowing who's doing it.

How about you? Have you found how you can best contribute to make a difference in your life and that of others? Remember, what you give unconditionally will be returned tenfold. That's just the way it works. Believe it!

"*There are thousands of stories of invention, medical discovery, business success, and individual achievement in all areas. Yet, the one factor common to all of them is that the person or persons accomplishing each feat believed in the possibility of it happening—before ever seeing the reality.*"

—John Fuhrman

LEADING LEADERS TO LEADERSHIP—*John Fuhrman*

Chapter Nineteen

Believe It Then You'll See It

"Faith is the daring of the soul to go further than it can see."
— William Newton Clark

omeone has to be first. In sports, records count for everything. Who has the most hits? Which team has the best record? Who scored more than anyone else? On and on it goes. Where do these records come from and what do they have to do with leadership?

For one thing, someone had to achieve something that some group acknowledged as significant. Until that achievement level is surpassed, there's no one new to recognize. The significance of the original record is often measured, or even enhanced, by the effort required from the subsequent record breaker. This may be through the new person's repeated attempts, failures, and final victory in his or her quest to be better than the best.

Up until the time Roger Banister had run a mile in under four minutes, most people thought it was impossible. But in the year following the feat, several others ran the mile in less than four minutes. Today, running a mile in anything *over* four minutes would probably disqualify you from official competition.

It wasn't until Bannister led the way and showed how to do it that the "impossible" became the new minimum standard. That's what leaders do. They demonstrate what can be accomplished and lead others to exceed that. They show others that previous accomplishments, while significant at the time, aren't always the ultimate.

Unfortunately, some leaders are insecure—they may try to destroy the validity of record breakers. Rather than strive to achieve more, they often focus on the faults of the winners and attribute outside positive factors to being responsible for their accomplishments. They endeavor to diminish the magnitude of the triumph or put down the person attempting the challenge. They may even go so far as to fail to recognize the accomplishment in any way. Their insecurity leads them to believe that they'll appear "less than" by noting the achievements or efforts of others.

With 95 percent of the population clinging to "just getting by," many seem to find comfort in bringing heroes down a few notches, rather than holding them and their victories up to encourage themselves and others. Many have fallen into the trap of becoming nothing more than a bunch of "Yes, buts." Every time someone accomplishes something above and beyond the norm, the majority of people typically find fault and downplay the accomplishments. They say, "Yes, but" then point out the fault. Or they may attribute the success to just luck and good fortune, rather than consistent focus and appropriate action.

Leaders realize that great accomplishments are made by overcoming weaknesses, setbacks, lack of belief, lack of money, put-downs by others, and a multitude of other obstacles. These "potholes" along the way don't deter them from grand feats. In most cases, hurdling the challenges helped them become who they are.

Succeeding in Spite of...

One thing that makes leaders stand out from the crowd is that they often do things and take paths in spite of what other people may think, say, or do. They make decisions based on their own wisdom, experiences, and the guidance from caring mentors. They are willing to grow. Most important, they are willing to courageously do this in front of others to increase their accountability and set an example.

Naysayers can't discourage achievement-oriented leaders. Their negativity actually encourages the winners to say "I'll show you." For example, one of the underlying motivations to finish and get my first book published was a negative boss. He told me that I'd never write a book or do anything else of value. I was determined to succeed in spite of what he thought. Frankly, the book turned out better because of his "motivation."

The best motivation often comes from those who keep telling you it can't be done. If all other resources seem to be failing, you can actually draw strength from the taunting of those who predict your failure. This could give you just enough extra go-power to get the job done. It can even stir you to take a new look at your situation as you persevere to find a way to make it work. Then watch those people say they knew you could do it!

Perfect Sight or *Clear Vision*

When you consider doing something new or doing things a different way, a new world opens up to you. If you focus on the history of your failed attempt, you will only find the avenues that didn't work. Dwell on it long enough and you can become an expert on why this idea won't work, instead of how it can be brought to fruition.

Your creative, solution-oriented vision is what lets you see the possibilities. It can also help you focus on the benefits of taking positive action. Set your sights on what your expanded vision tells you is possible. Then focus on helping others in the process. This will keep you tuned in to making the necessary adjustments to reach your destination.

Relative to what is possible to achieve, most people have very limited vision. That may sound a bit negative, but read on and see if you agree. While there are limits to each person's vision, I am also convinced that most of us never come close to reaching them. Let's take a look at how your vision may be limited.

Have you ever thought about curing a disease? I certainly haven't. How about envisioning the discovery of a new species of animal or even encountering a new, unexplored territory? Not me. Yet, long before I ever wrote my first book, I had the vision of seeing my name on the cover.

Our brains are complex but user friendly. Within our own limitations, our brains will not allow us to think of anything that we, as individuals or in concert with others, aren't capable of accomplishing.

Nearly 70 years ago, Napoleon Hill, author and researcher of success, wrote, "Whatever the mind can conceive and believe it can achieve." So, if there is an idea that keeps popping up in your mind, you may want to take a long hard look at the possibility of achieving it. It could be part of the vision of what you are meant to do. What if the Wright brothers had ignored their vision of flying?

A vision of what can be always needs to occur before we can accomplish something. It's the starting point of all achievement. The exciting vision of what we seek to accomplish keeps us going through the challenges and adversities that accompany any effort to change our current reality. Vision allows us to see beyond the obstacles to the golden objectives. Leaders have vision.

If all you believe in is what you can physically see, your life is out of your control. For example, does advertising, true or false, rule what you purchase? Will the news dictate the type of day you will have? Will you lose hope of a brighter future? Will others control your destiny? If you answered yes to any of these questions, you are surviving without the benefit of having a creative, fulfilling life. You'll be a reactor, instead of the proactive inventor of your life and the fine leader you aspire to be.

With a vision, that is, a dream or objective for your future, you begin to feel you have hold of worthy purpose for being here. You have hope there is something beyond the next obstacle, besides more of the same routine.

Too many people have the goal of making it to payday. Unfortunately, that doesn't lead to grander accomplishments or a richer, more meaningful life experience. That's all they're focusing on, so that's what they're getting.

Once someone sees beyond the day-to-day grind and discovers a reason to work toward something worthy of striving for, the day-to-day difficulties become a minute part of the bigger picture. Life becomes purposeful. The focus is toward extraordinary accomplishment, rather than on looking back in regret at what could have been.

Believe in Everyone—*But Count on No One*

Effective leaders develop the ability to help others stretch toward what they believe is their fullest potential, and then encourage them to do just a little more. Once they accomplish that, a new level of potential is established—and the next level comes into view. The journey becomes an ascending spiral. Encouraging others to realize and maximize their potential is a true leadership quality. It requires the courage to accept that they may be able to reach heights you have yet to reach, while sadly others will not follow through. It's impossible to *make* someone else succeed. The old adage, "You can lead a horse to water, but you can't make him drink," still applies. A leader-to-be will give you signs—he or she will ask for your help and take your lead.

Often the easiest way to empower others to do new things is to have a strong belief in their ability to accomplish the tasks. Some of my biggest accomplishments and successes came after others believed I could do it. This was especially true whenever my self-belief had been shaken.

Leaders who are constantly helping others succeed often find themselves being supported when they most need it. True leaders also understand the importance of teamwork in achieving any endeavor. They realize that no matter how much help they accept, though, their positions as leaders are never diminished—they're actually strengthened. A leader surrounds him or herself with competent leaders-to-be— those who want to lead.

The difference between an amateur leader and a professional one is that the professional knows when to seek the help of his or her leaders-to-be and readily does so. While successful leaders receive help along the way, their ultimate success is determined by consistently helping others as they seek to make a mark in the world.

It Makes Perfect Sense

Have you or has anyone you know ever witnessed something seemingly appearing out of thin air? Has something fallen into your lap that was exactly what you needed at the time?

When you began to think about what you needed and did some work toward it, did you notice that it often came to pass? It almost seems like magic. However, anything is possible when you first think about it, then apply yourself toward making it happen. Consider any great invention.

Take the electric light bulb. Edison just didn't wake up one day, casually flip a switch, and magically notice the room filled with light. He didn't invent the light bulb and then devise a plan as to how it would come to be. That would have been backwards. Life doesn't work that way.

At some point, a thought, a possibility, or even a dream began to grow in Edison's mind. This, no doubt, occurs in other people's minds as well, before anything new is invented. Edison believed what he imagined could be made to happen, and he committed to doing whatever it took to make it so. He even considered the probability of failure and welcomed it as the way of discovering what wouldn't work and making adjustments.

There are thousands of stories of inventions, medical discoveries, business successes, and individual achievements in all areas. Yet, the one factor common to all of them is that the person or persons accomplishing each feat believed in the possibility of it happening—before it was a reality.

When you accept the idea that envisioning something first is essential to creating it physically, then you are ready to begin looking at the possibilities open to you in all areas of your job, business, or life. Whatever thoughts come into your head are what's possible for you. Isn't that exciting? When you allow your dreams or visions to grow so strong that the picture becomes crystal clear, you open yourself up to the real potential in store for you.

Realizing your own potential, day by day, is the first step toward a life filled with magnificent possibilities, rather than an existence of nothing more than making a living. It opens up a life of quality and richness. Begin believing you can bring your vision to reality, then lead others to help you make it happen.

"To find a leader, you need to be a leader. Act as if you are the type of leader for whom you are looking. Once you start establishing leadership qualities and habits, you'll begin attracting others who will follow your lead."

—John Fuhrman

Chapter Twenty

Complicated Might Seem Better, But Simpler Is Faster

"In character, in manners, in style, in all things, the supreme excellence is simplicity."

— Longfellow

If you were walking down the street and a man was coming toward you with a huge smile, how would you feel? When you asked him the often obligatory, "How are you?" and got a reply like, "Outstanding! Things couldn't be better," how would you react?

A little farther down the block, another man approaches you mumbling, "Life is awful. I never get any breaks. The economy is bad and I'll probably get laid off."

Who's telling the truth?

Probably both of them. In their own minds, they are being truthful. However, many people believe that the one who says he is miserable is the honest one. They think the positive one is hiding something or choosing to ignore reality. For some reason, it is difficult for some people to accept the authenticity of a person who is honestly happy with where he or she is in life. The perception is often that the one who is miserable is the one who is really working hard. Anyone who is that happy might be perceived as shiftless and lazy—or at least avoiding reality.

When asked how anyone could be so happy, the reply is often simple. That person has a positive attitude and looks forward to each day as an opportunity to reach more of his or her potential. However, most people aren't satisfied with such an answer.

Conversely, what happens if we ask someone why he or she feels so miserable? Be prepared for a lengthy dissertation on the faults of others who have caused this person to have his or her lot in life. That individual may even explore the complexities of global events and how it all relates to where he or she is. Unfortunately, after a long whining session, the tendency is to accept the negative answers as real because of the conviction of the speaker and the complexity involved.

Comfort in the Complex

Every living creature is incredibly complex in its makeup, yet often simple in its actions. Bees land on flowers and take pollen to other flowers, helping them grow. The bees then go back to their hives and make honey. We enjoy the beauty of the garden and the sweetness of honey but all the bee did was instinctively fly from place to place.

Ego is a unique human characteristic. Some people are so wrapped up with the idea that we are the superior species that simple answers just aren't enough. They want more to satisfy their intelligent nature. The more complicated the answers, especially the negative ones, the better they feel about hearing them. They may say, "Well, that makes sense," when confronted with the opportunity to respond to a negatively-presented story.

Can you remember being in your place of worship as a child? Everything on the earth was a marvel of simplicity. For example, why is the sky blue? That's the way God made it. Simple.

Stealing from someone is a crime. Simple, right? However, in today's criminal justice system, we first analyze the circumstances. We then take a look at the environment in which the person was raised. Finally, we weigh it against how others in similar situations have been handled. It's no longer simple. But, in our current state of affairs, it is seemingly much more acceptable. Not taking responsibility for our errors, regardless of obviousness of fault—a victim mentality—is frequently the norm.

Leaders, however, *can* choose simplicity. They can blast through the so-called complicated issues, which are often used as a smokescreen for what's really happening, and arrive at a direct and simple solution. They then need to be courageous enough to share that solution regardless of how others might react, and be first in line to take the appropriate action to make it happen.

The finest business leaders demonstrate this incredibly well. The super-successful of this admirable group became billionaires by simplifying the complex.

Sam Walton rewrote the rules on distribution when he created Wal-Mart, and became one of the wealthiest men on the planet. Ross Perot found a more direct way of exchanging information, simplified it, and became wealthy enough to run for President of the United States—using his own money. There are many others who also have been able to accomplish significant levels of success by simplifying the way things get done.

What amazes these leaders is how the rest of the world looks in awe, marveling at the simplicity. The best leaders always look first for the simplest solution. They thrive on simplicity and teach those around them to do the same.

You may be asking yourself, "How do I find the simplest solution to any given challenge?"

First, gather the facts, then ask for suggestions from those involved and, if needed, from the person leading you. Then decide the fairest, simplest thing to do, all things considered. For example, if the challenge lies in the feuding of two employees or associates, it may require bringing the parties together in a supervised setting to discuss the issues. Once everything is out on the table, it may require an apology from the person whose stress level leads him or her to blow up at the other. It could be as simple as that.

Make Yourself Simply Uncomfortable

When you want to get in shape after a long layoff from physical activity, what does it feel like after the first day of exercise? Don't you feel tightness in your muscles and a bit of pain? Of course. But that's just part of the necessary progression on the road back to physical fitness.

Leadership is similar. If you are used to wading through piles of information on the way things have always been done, it's uncomfortable to present a simple solution, especially the first time. You may believe it won't look like you did your job. You'll probably feel tight and uneasy as you present your thoughts. However, once you mentally stretch yourself, your mind can never shrink back to its original size. That's how leaders grow.

The discomfort felt in the growth process is often caused by the confusion between simple and easy. Many have been conditioned to believe that those two words mean the same thing. But they are not at all alike—especially in discovering solutions and birthing new ideas.

A simple solution often means it is readily understood and not made up of many parts. Getting from point A to point B may not be a straight line, and simple solutions are seldom easy. They usually require a great deal of effort and persistence. To come up with a simple solution may take more thought, to chunk the problem down to its core.

Complicated solutions seem to have a built-in safety valve for failure. The person who came up with it can always say that the idea was so complicated that failing was a good possibility. A simple solution, however, doesn't lend itself to that excuse. There is no turning back. There simply isn't anything in the plan that can be blamed for it not succeeding other than, perhaps, a lack of sticktoitiveness.

Every aspect of growth creates some discomfort. This happens with anything that is stretched beyond its current size—in this case, beyond the present mode of operation.

However, the benefits of stretching are invaluable—whether or not the task was successfully completed. Personally and professionally, you'll grow as a leader—as someone who can relate to and attract people at a higher level of development. Certain others will look at your efforts and recognize your leadership abilities, regardless of the outcome of any particular venture. This is especially true if you don't arrive at the desired destination, but immediately begin rallying the troops for a second round. Your bounce-back ability will be evident. You'll also realize that your growth is determined by how often and how far you go beyond where you've been comfortable operating in the past.

Simplifying things for those around you takes more initial effort as you determine what's really essential to be done. There's no longer the dragging on of a project or endeavor because it's so complicated that it requires an army of committees and endless hours of deliberation. This approach generates new ideas, uncluttered by the anchors of bureaucratic-entrenched "safety." It may encounter resistance, as change generally does, but the cost effectiveness and stress-reducing aspects make dealing with it worthwhile.

Remember, failure is simply an event. It can't stop us unless we let events control our lives, and we gauge our future efforts on them as barometers of what we can do. Simple, unburdened solutions provide a more direct path to success, but poorly-thought-out solutions are open invitations for failure.

Simple? Yes. Easy? Not necessarily. Our familiarity with taking the easy way out has often prevented us from taking advantage of simple solutions that would lead us to the better life we say we want. Easy becomes a way of life that is harder in the long-run because it's the path that leads to an average life. The rich experience of striving for our heartfelt dreams and objectives is missing. It's the regretful path of "I only wish I had...." Easy diminishes the value we put on things. Easy follows the crowd, but the crowd rarely has exciting, purpose-filled lives.

Exemplary leaders acknowledge but kindly decline complicated solutions. They embrace simple solutions, but they don't take the easy way out. This alone separates them from the masses, who are living on future borrowed dollars, ignoring the uninspiring life that awaits them. Their commitment in seeking simple solutions to challenges, as well as creating win-win relationships, soon starts turning heads and generating respect. By working with these simple ideas and achieving what you want, you can lead others to their own levels of success. In short, see it big, but keep it simple.

Chapter Twenty-One

Spend Less Time Looking and More Time Leading

"People want to follow only those who know where they are going and are headed in the right direction."

— Anonymous

When people first go into business, they are usually told that in order to be successful, they need to surround themselves with a few key people. Great advice, but many believe the *only* thing they need to do is to find some successful people, and then sit back and watch success happen. This is shortsighted and only leads to disappointment.

Basically, there are four categories of people you can surround yourself with: 1) Those who are extremely successful in their current endeavors but, for some reason, want to make a change; 2) Those who have some success in their current endeavors, but would like to improve upon it; 3) Those who have yet to achieve any success beyond average, but would like to do so; and 4) Those who have no ambition or desire to accomplish anything more.

To enhance your chances of success, the people you choose to have associate with you need to have a dream and be at or above your level of thinking. However, no matter what level of success people may have achieved in their respective fields of endeavor, they still need to be humble enough to be good followers when they get into a new field. They need to appreciate, learn from, and apply the experience and wisdom of those already successful in that field. They also need to accept the strong and, hopefully, compassionate guidance of role models who can help them envision their dreams and objectives, and show them how to become leaders in the new field.

Accepting new leadership, no matter what the leader's age or background may be, is essential for an aspiring leader's success in any new field. If they refuse the leadership of those who came before them, perhaps because they let pride or ego get in the way, they will fail in the new line of business.

So what can want-to-be leaders in a new field possibly do to help their newcomers become leaders? They first need to lead them to the leaders who can show them what to do. They can begin their leadership roles simply by introducing (leading) their new people to the leaders in the new arena. Then, as they grow in their own leadership abilities, they'll have other new people introducing *their* newcomers to *them*!

The most competent leaders in any field of endeavor are first good followers. But, nevertheless, leadership is taken not given. Those who really want to lead *take* the lead. Leaders lead! They don't wait until they "know it all," or the "crown of leader" is bestowed upon them by someone else. They go with what they have, learn all they can in the process, and start leading. Even if they believe no one is paying attention to them at the moment, they travel steadily toward their goals, setting the example for others to follow. They're self-motivated.

So what's the best way to find a leader? Simple. To find a leader you need to *be* a leader. And what's the best way to fire yourself up to start becoming a leader? You need to have a strong dream, vision, or objective, and be passionate about it, before anyone will want to follow you.

Then, you need to start acting *as if!* Act as if you are the type of leader for whom you are looking. Act as if you have all the qualities you would like to see in other leaders. When you habitually act as if, you will develop new behaviors. Once you start establishing leadership qualities and habits, you'll begin *attracting* others who will follow your lead.

You may be amazed at the number of leaders you'll begin attracting into your life. They will enhance your company or organization, as well as challenge your understanding and skills, helping you grow to the next level of leadership and success.

Begin creating an enthusiastic, productive leadership team by having a positive, assumptive attitude. Act as if your team already exists. Think about what you will accomplish, and act as if it has already occurred. Smile as if you are on the cutting edge of a new beginning—because you are! People are attracted to success, so act successful. Consider it to be the truth in advance. Keep acting successful and you'll become successful.

There's an expression that sums up this assumptive attitude that many people don't understand: "Fake it 'til you make it." Many think this is being deceptive. For a long time I did too. But I found that when you create the feeling you expect to have when you reach your goals—before you reach them— you can attract all the people you need to help you reach them. It just becomes another self-fulfilling prophecy. But always remember, the only way for you to become truly successful is for you to help (lead) others to get what they want.

I did this to keep myself going when I was writing my first book. Things were tight, and I hadn't even found a publisher. My kids were just entering private schools with tuition that had to be paid. The stress on my wife was starting to show.

The response pattern I chose was to have the attitude that everything was alright until I could make it better.

Instead of talking about bills and how bad things were, I began to talk to the kids about going to Disney World. I started sharing with my wife all the things we'd be doing after the book was released. Then the transformation began. Hope was restored. My wife and kids began believing in my ability to create a brighter future, and they were starting to get excited about all the possibilities.

I also became more enthusiastic, and my belief level soared. I developed a sense of urgency, began writing faster, and more creativity kicked in. I put together some speaking programs based on my sales experiences, and began contacting companies and organizations about what I could do for them. Shortly, they began hiring me to speak, and my business began to accelerate—even though the book was yet to be published. Once it was finally in print, the opportunities to help others began to multiply.

You'll be amazed at what can happen when you have more faith in yourself and passionately share your dreams and objectives with others. Once they understand that you are committed to your goals, and you have a good sense of what it will be like when you accomplish them, others are more likely to support you—while still others may become a part of the process. This is the turning point when you begin to attract the help you need to achieve your objective.

The simpler you keep things, the faster you can grow as a leader. Make kindness, simplicity, positive attitude, and vision your mainstays. These qualities help you encourage accelerated success in others and, in turn, yourself. After all, no one has forever. And as I've often heard leaders say...

"*The pace of the pack is determined by the speed of the leader.*"

An Open Letter to Leaders in Training

Dear Leader,

You are special. You may have heard that before, but maybe you didn't quite believe. Let me share something that will prove why it's so.

First of all, congratulations for completing this book. Why is that so important? The truth is, many people buy only one book a year. You may say, this is the only one you bought so how are you special? You finished the book! Incredibly, of all the books purchased, most are read only through the first chapter. Doing what others won't do is a sure sign of leadership.

You may not consider yourself much of an expert on leadership. That's okay. Do what I do—passionately observe those who are more proficient at leadership than you are. Emulate them and follow in their footsteps. Share what you've learned to help others—which will reinforce your grasp of the new knowledge and embrace your position as a leader. Taking action on those ideas will attract others into your life who will either follow your example or lead you to the next level. Be humble, open-minded, and action-oriented. Ask for what you need from your leaders to guide you to the level of success that reflects more of your true potential.

To be a leader you first need to establish your position as a leader in your own life. As you accomplish more of your goals and objectives, stay alert to opportunities to mentor others who would appreciate your assistance in achieving their own levels of leadership excellence. This is not only an enjoyable and wonderful way to give back, but you will also become a finer, stronger leader in the process. As a result, you'll soon find yourself leading leaders to leadership.

Continued Success,

John Fuhrman

Who Is John Fuhrman?

Since the release of his first book in 1997, John Fuhrman has reached over one million people with his ideas and programs. He speaks both in the United States and abroad, and his books have been translated into several foreign languages. He is an award-winning member of the National Speakers Association and has served on the board of his local chapter. He has been interviewed countless times in the media across the United States.

John's teachings have been published in numerous magazines, where he has been featured as an expert on success strategies and overcoming the fears of failure and rejection. His words of wisdom also appear on various Internet sites.

He has presented his messages to various fields of endeavor, including health care, sales, technology, corporate, and direct sales and network marketing organizations. John compels each of his audiences to take action with a few simple steps. The results speak for themselves.

John lives in New Hampshire with his wife Helen and his son John and daughter Katie.